Robert Wilson

Boiler and factory chimneys, their draught-power and stability

With a chapter on lightning conductors

Robert Wilson

Boiler and factory chimneys, their draught-power and stability
With a chapter on lightning conductors

ISBN/EAN: 9783744715294

Printed in Europe, USA, Canada, Australia, Japan

Cover: Foto ©Andreas Hilbeck / pixelio.de

More available books at **www.hansebooks.com**

TABLE OF DIMENSIONS OF CHIMNEYS.

On the basis of the head of outside air being equal to half the height of Chimney, and the flues being not much over six times the length of boiler.

Height of Chimney in feet.	$W = \dfrac{A\sqrt{H}}{\cdot07} =$ lbs. of coal per hour per 1 foot of area at top of Chimney.	$H_0 = 0\cdot192\ H^{\frac{1}{2}}(\cdot0761) =$ height in inches of column of water balanced by draught pressure.	$HP = \dfrac{A\sqrt{H}}{\cdot75} =$ Horse power of each sq.ft. of Chimney. Assuming 7 lbs. of coal per horse power.	$A = \dfrac{\cdot3}{\sqrt{H}} =$ area of top per H.P. Chimney in feet per H.P. for 1 or 2 boilers.	$A = \dfrac{\cdot5}{\sqrt{H}} =$ area of top of Chimney in ft. per H.P. where several boilers are working together.	$A = \dfrac{1\cdot}{\sqrt{H}} =$ area of flue in feet per horse power.
30	78·24	·218	7·3	·146	091	·182
40	90·35	·296	8·4	126	·077	·155
50	101·01	·364	9·4	·113	·070	·140
60	110·65	·437	10·3	·103	·064	·129
70	119·52	·5	11·2	·095	·059	·119
80	127·77	·58	11·9	·089	·055	·111
90	135·52	·656	12·6	·084	·052	·105
100	142·85	·729	13·3	·08	·05	·01
125	159·71	·911	14·9	·071	·044	·089
150	174·96	1·09	16·3	·065	·04	·082
175	188·98	1·26	17·6	·060	·038	·075
200	202·03	1·45	18·8	·056	·035	·07
225	214·28	1·64	20	·053	·033	·066
250	225·87	1·82	21	·05	·031	·063
275	236·90	1·99	22	·048	·03	·06
300	247·43	2·18	23	·046	·028	·057

When the area at top is given as in fifth and sixth columns, the dimension of the side of square in a square chimney can easily be found by taking the square root of the area, or side of square $= \sqrt{A}$, and the diameter for a round chimney $= \sqrt{\dfrac{A}{\cdot7854}}$. See p. 30.

BOILER AND FACTORY CHIMNEYS,

THEIR DRAUGHT-POWER AND STABILITY:

WITH A CHAPTER ON

LIGHTNING CONDUCTORS.

BY

ROBERT WILSON, A.I.C.E.,

AUTHOR OF "TREATISE ON STEAM BOILERS," "COMMON SENSE FOR GAS
USERS," ETC., ETC

Fourth Edition.

Capio Lumen

LONDON:
CROSBY LOCKWOOD & SON,
7, STATIONERS' HALL COURT, LUDGATE HILL.
1899.

BRADBURY, AGNEW, & CO. LD., PRINTERS,
LONDON AND TONBRIDGE.

PREFACE.

THE following Chapters were commenced with the intention of adding them to the 5th Edition of my "Treatise on Steam Boilers," in consequence of having had numerous enquiries respecting the proper size of chimney for boiler-work. The information is, however, likely to be more useful in its present form, hence the appearance of this little book.

I had some diffidence in calling in question the correctness of the theory of draught adopted by Rankine, by Morin, and by Peclet in the 2nd Edition of his "Traité de la Chaleur," but after going to press I find that Peclet in the 3rd Edition of his work has altered his theory and adopted the same as I have arrived at.

ROBERT WILSON.

CONTENTS.

—◆—

BOILER AND FACTORY CHIMNEYS.

CHAPTER I.

CHIMNEY DRAUGHT.

BOILER chimneys are used not only in order to obtain a sufficient flow of air to maintain a steady combustion, but also to discharge the noxious gases of combustion at such a height above the ground that they shall not be considered a nuisance.

It is well known that the pressure of a fluid is equal in all directions, and is measured at any given point by the area, density, and height above that point of the column of liquid or gas which exerts the pressure.

In fig. 1, let $A B = C D$ represent the height of the atmosphere, and $D F$ the height of a chimney. Then the pressure on the top of the column of air in the chimney is measured by $C F$, and the pressure on the bottom of the same column by $C F + F D$. When the temperature and density of the column $F D$ inside the chimney are the same as those of a column $E B$ of equal height and area outside, it is evident that the two columns $A E + E B$ and $C F + F D$ will be in equilibrio, and there will be no tendency to produce motion. Should, however, the column $F D$ inside the chimney be of a higher temperature and consequently of less density than a column $E B$ of equal height and

B

area outside, the weight of the column $A E + E B$ will

Fig. 1.

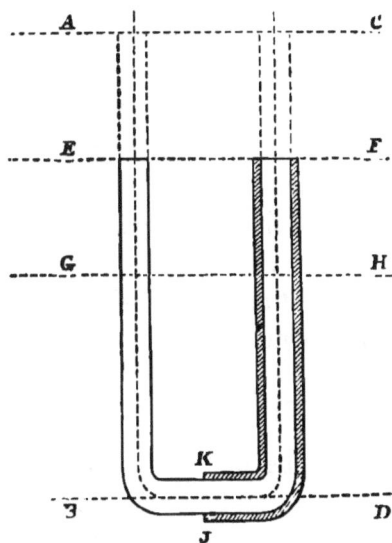

be greater than that of $C F + F D$, whence the preponderating pressure at $J K$ will force the inside column $F D$ upwards. If the air, as it passes $J K$, becomes heated, and the diminished density of the column inside the chimney is maintained, the column will continue to be forced upwards by the unbalanced pressure outside.

This is what takes place when a fire is lighted under a chimney, and the continuous current of cold air, that forces the heated and lighter air upwards, produces what is called the draught, which is the name given (wrongly) to the quantity of heated gas discharged by the chimney, whether expressed by weight or volume of the gases ; or the velocity of the current ; or by the pressure required to produce that current. It is evident that the force of the draught will depend upon the difference in the weight of the two columns $A E + E B$ and $C F + F D$. Now as $A E$ and $C F$, the height of the portions of the columns above the chimney, are equal, they balance each other, and may be left out of consideration for the present.

Assuming the temperature of the atmosphere to be 62°—a fair average—then every additional degree of heat imparted to the air would increase its bulk $\frac{1}{523}$ or, by increasing its temperature by 523 degrees, its volume would be doubled, and its density consequently reduced by one-half.

Let $D = 0.0761$, the density or weight of a cubic foot of the outside air at 62° ;

$d =$ the density of the hot gas in the chimney, assumed to be constant from the bridge to the chimney-top ;

$t =$ the temperature of the hot gas in the chimney ;

then the density d of the hot gas at any required temperature t, can be found by the formula

$$d = \cdot 0761 \left(\frac{523}{461 + t} \right).$$

If we represent the weight of the heated column by $D H$ in fig. 1, $F H = E G$ will represent the difference in weight or pressure between the two columns $F D$ and $E B$.

Let $H =$ the height of the chimney;

$P =$ the difference in pressure between the two columns ;

then $P = H D - H d = H (D - d)$.

This unbalanced pressure P is the motive force which drives the hot-air up the chimney, and the height in feet of a column of the external air or *"head"* H_1 *in feet of cold air*, to produce this pressure, acting by its own weight, is found by dividing P by the density of the external air, whence

$$H_1 = \frac{P}{D} = \frac{H (D - d)}{D}$$

This head H_1 is represented graphically on fig. 1 by $F H = E G$, as before.

If we take, for example, a chimney 90 ft. high, in which the volume of the air is doubled in passing through the fire, we shall have $D = 0.0761$ and $d = 0.0380$, whence

$$H_1 = 90 \left(\frac{.0761 - .0380}{.0761} \right) = 90(\tfrac{1}{2}) = 45 \text{ ft.}$$

The head is proportional to the height of the chimney.

When we know

  $t =$ the temperature of the chimney gases above zero;

  $T =$ the temperature of the atmosphere;

  $a =$ the coefficient of expansion of air for one degree of the thermometer at zero $= 0.00217$;

we have

$$H_1 = H \left(\frac{D - d}{D} \right) = a \left(\frac{t - T}{1 + a\,t} \right) H.$$

Taking $t_1 =$ the temperature of the gases above that of the atmosphere at $62°$, which makes $T = 62°$, we have the following simple rule

$$H_1 = \frac{t_1}{523 + t_1} H.$$

Suppose the temperature of the gas inside the chimney to be $500°$, then

  $t_1 = 600° - 62° = 538°$, and

$$H_1 = \frac{538}{1061} H = 0.574, \text{ or very nearly one half the}$$

height of the chimney.

When the head is known, the theoretical mean velocity per second with which the external air tends to enter the chimney can easily be calculated. Supposing the chimney were quite empty, and there were no loss by contraction at entrance, then, if a column of outside air were allowed to descend into it by its own weight, the velocity which the column would acquire by the time its top reached the entrance into the chimney would be that due to the height the column had fallen, which would be equal to the height of the chimney, and the velocity of the entering air would be $= \sqrt{2\,g\,\mathrm{H}} = 8\sqrt{\mathrm{H}}$, $2\,g$ being twice the velocity produced by gravity in the first second of fall.

But the chimney is never quite empty, and the height of the column to which the theoretical velocity, v, in feet per second, of the entering cold air is due, becomes equal to the square root of the height of the head H_{ι} or the theoretical velocity of the cold air,—

$$v = \sqrt{2\,g\,\mathrm{H}\frac{\mathrm{D}-d}{\mathrm{D}}} = 8\sqrt{\mathrm{H}\frac{\mathrm{D}-d}{\mathrm{D}}}$$

$$v = 8\sqrt{\mathrm{H}\,a\frac{(t-\mathrm{T})}{1+at}} = 8\sqrt{\mathrm{H}\frac{t_1}{523+t_1}}$$

$$= 8\sqrt{\mathrm{H}_1}.$$

Suppose the head of cold air $\mathrm{H}_{\iota} = \cdot5\,\mathrm{H}$ and $\mathrm{H} = 90$, then $v = 8\sqrt{45} = 53{\cdot}7$.

On passing through the fire the air is increased in *volume* in proportion to the increase of temperature, but not by the amount of the bulk of the gases it enters into combination with (see p. 19). The velocity, therefore, of the heated air will be much greater than that of the entering cold air.

As the velocity of the gases is proportional to their volumes, we have for V, the theoretical velocity of the hot air in the chimney,

$$\mathrm{V} = v\left(\frac{461+t}{523}\right) = 8\sqrt{\mathrm{H}_1}\left(\frac{461+t}{523}\right) = 8\sqrt{\mathrm{H}_1}\times\frac{\mathrm{D}}{d}.$$

Peclet, Rankine, and Morin have all taken the

head, in feet of *hot gas*, or $h_1 = H_1 \dfrac{D}{d}$ and make

$V = \sqrt{2\,G\,H\,\dfrac{D-d}{d}}$. This is evidently an error, since

$\sqrt{\dfrac{D-d}{d}}$ is not equal to $\dfrac{D}{d}\sqrt{\dfrac{D-d}{D}}$. The velocity of
the hot gases is always dependent in the first place upon
the velocity of the entering cold air, and consequently
upon H_1 and not upon the head of hot gas h_1.

If $Q = $ volume of gases discharged per second by
  the chimney ;

$A = $ area of chimney ; we have

$$Q = V\,A = A\,8\sqrt{H\dfrac{D-d}{D}} \times \dfrac{D}{d} = A\,8\sqrt{H_1} \times \dfrac{D}{d}$$

$$= A\,8\sqrt{H\,a\dfrac{(t-T)}{1+at}} \times \dfrac{461+t}{523.}$$

From the foregoing it is evident that the theoretical
velocity and volume of the hot gas discharged from the
chimney are proportional to *the square root of the
height of the chimney ; to the square root of the head
or excess of pressure of the outside air over that of the
hot gas in the chimney;* or to the square root of the
increase of temperature of the hot gas.

An error made by some writers on this subject is in
assuming that because $V = \dfrac{D}{d}v$ the draught force
increases in proportion to the increase in velocity or
inversely as the increase in density of the heated gases.
But as the motive force, or force that produces the
draught, is proportional to the height of the head,
and the velocity due to this head is proportional
to the square root of its height or to $\sqrt{H_1}$, and

as this height is proportional to the ratio of the densities, or to $\dfrac{D-d}{D}$ we have the velocity proportionate to $\sqrt{\dfrac{D-d}{D}}$ and not to $\dfrac{D}{d}$.

The actual velocity of the entering cold air and hot gases is reduced below the theoretical velocity by the resistance to their passage offered by the contracted areas through the fire-grate and layer of fuel, and over the bridge, by the bends and change of direction in the flues, by the change of shape and area of flues which cause eddies in the current, and by the friction against the sides of the flues and chimney.

Let $\dfrac{1}{K}$ express the relation of these various resistances to the velocity of the hot gases, then we shall have

$$V = \frac{1}{K} \sqrt{2 \, G \, H_1 \times \frac{D}{d}}.$$

According to Peclet's researches the actual velocity is given approximately by the following formula.

$$V = 8\left(\frac{461+t}{523}\right) \sqrt{\frac{H}{1 + G + \left(\dfrac{fl}{4} + N\right)\left(1 + at\right)^2}}$$

here $l=$ the whole length of chimney and flues, in feet;

$f=$ a co-efficient of friction which Peclet found to be 0·012 for the passage of furnace gases over sooty surfaces;

$d=$ diameter of round, or side of square flues;

$G=$ a factor of resistance for the passage of air through the grate and the layer of fuel above it, which may be taken at 40 for ordinary Boiler furnaces.

$N=$ number of bends at right angles to direction of current.

Morin, who has wrongly, as we consider, assumed the velocity of the hot gas to vary as $\sqrt{\dfrac{D-d}{d}}$ instead of $\sqrt{\dfrac{D-d}{D}} \times \dfrac{D}{d}$, gives the following method of investigating the forms of resistance theoretically, the co-efficients being our own:—It is evident that the moving force P, which tends to make the air enter the chimney is expressed by

$$P = (D-d)\,A\,H$$

A being the area of the chimney as before. If the mean velocity of the current in the chimney be V, the work developed per second by the motive pressure will be

$$(D - d)\,A\,H\,V.$$

The resistance of the sides to the movement of the gases will be represented by the expression

$$\frac{d\,S\,L\,\beta\,V^2}{g.}$$

S being the perimeter, or contour of the flues or chimney; L, the length of the chimney and flues, being equal to H when vertical; β, a co-efficient for any given kind of internal surface of flues and chimney.

The work developed per second by this resistance will be

$$\frac{d\,S\,L\,\beta\,V^3}{g.}$$

If $M = \dfrac{W}{g}$ the mass of the gases, whose weight $W = d\,A\,V$, the *vis viva* imparted to this mass by the difference of pressures or motive force P will be

$$M\,V^2$$

Now this *vis viva* is usually diminished in at least six different modes :—

1. By the contraction at the entrance of the ash-pit. Now, supposing this entrance to be equal in area to the flues, the loss of *vis viva* may be expressed by

$$M\left(\frac{1}{m}-1\right)^2 V^2$$

m being the co-efficient of contraction at entrance. This loss of *vis viva* may be neglected when the orifice of entrance is such that m differs very little from unity ; but this is seldom the case. The co-efficient m of contraction is usually taken from 0·60 to 0·80. Taking it at 0·70, we have

$$\left(\frac{1}{m}-1\right)^2 = \left(\frac{1}{\cdot70}-1\right)^2 = \cdot185.$$

The total *vis viva* given to the gases in motion, and which consists of that maintained in the chimney and of that lost at the entrance, will be expressed by

$$M\left(+ \ \left(\frac{1}{m}-1\right)^2\right) V^2$$

2. If the area of the entrance orifice has a section different from and less than that of the flues or chimney, the loss of *vis viva* will be M $(V'-V)^2$ $= M \ V'^2\left(\frac{A}{m'\,A'}-1\right)^2$, V' being the velocity through the orifice whose area is A'.

The term $\left(\frac{A}{m'\,A'}-1\right)^2$ may acquire a considerable value when all the air has to pass through the bars and bed of fuel and over the bridge. The area for the passage of air being frequently only $\frac{1}{10}$ the area of the section A of the chimney (or less when a thick layer of caking coal is used), in this case

$$\frac{A}{m' A'} = 10$$

and

$$\left(\frac{A}{m' A'} - 1\right)^2 = 81.$$

When the area for the passage of air through the fuel equals the space between the fire bars or commonly ½ the section of chimney outlet, then

$$\frac{A}{m' A'} = 2$$

and

$$\left(\frac{A}{m' A'} - 1\right)^2 = 1.$$

This formula is, strictly speaking, only applicable where the density of the fluid does not change in its passage.

3. A loss of *vis viva* takes place at every elbow or bend. With a single flush-flued externally fired boiler there may be only a single elbow, namely at the bottom of the chimney; but in tubular boilers set in the best manner and connected with a single chimney there are often as many as eight elbows. Taking this number, and expressing the loss at each bend by $M\left(\frac{1}{m''} - 1\right)^2 V^2$ we have to repeat the term $\left(\frac{1}{m} - 1\right)^2$ eight times. Supposing m″=0·70, we have

$$8\left(\frac{1}{m''} - 1\right)^2 = 8\left(\frac{1}{\cdot 70} - 1\right)^2 = 1\cdot48.$$

A similar loss occurs where two or more currents meet us in a split draught, uniting again in a single flue.

4. Then we have the loss of each enlargement of the

flue represented by $M\left(1 - \dfrac{A}{0}\right)^2 V^2$. This nearly
always occurs at the bridge, at the entrance of the flues
into the chimney, and where a number of tubes deliver
into a large space or flue. The greatest value this term
can have is in the case where the area 0 of the enlarged
section is so large in proportion to that A of the small
flue, or tube, that we may regard $\dfrac{A}{0} = 0$. Then

$$\left(1 - \frac{A}{0}\right)^2 = 1.$$

Supposing $\dfrac{A}{0} = \frac{1}{2}$ then

$$\left(1 - \frac{A}{0}\right)^2 = 0\cdot 25.$$

5. When the area A_1 of the exit orifice of the
chimney is less than the area A, the velocity will be
V_1 instead of V making the co-efficient of contraction
m_1 the volume of the gases discharged will be

$$m_1 A_1 V_1 = A V,$$

$$\text{whence } V_1 = \frac{A}{m_1 A_1} V.$$

when $m_1 A_1$ is less than A_1 the velocity V will be
greater than V, which will give a greater steadiness of
draught but diminish the volume discharged per second.
Taking the velocity of exit orifice to that of mean
velocity as 3 to 2, we have $V_1 = \dfrac{3}{2} V = 1\cdot 5\ V,$

$$\text{whence } \left(\frac{A}{m_1 A_1}\right)^2 = 2\cdot 25.$$

In tapered boiler chimneys the area A is usually
taken as that of the outlet, and in such cases the *vis*

viva becomes $M V_1^2$ instead of $M V^2$, and is not the average velocity of the draught in the chimney.

6. The resistance arising from the friction of the air or gases over the sooty surface of the flues and chimney will be represented by $\dfrac{2\,S\,L\,\beta}{A}$ as already given.

In a circular or square chimney we have $\dfrac{S}{A} = \dfrac{4}{D}$ this term then becomes

$$\frac{8\,L\,\beta}{D}$$

The value of the co-efficient β depends upon the number and shape of tubes, flues and passages through which the gases flow, and is given by Peclet as $0\cdot012$ for sooty surfaces.

The proportion $\dfrac{L}{D}$ varies very much, taking it at 100 and 30 respectively, the term $\dfrac{8\,L\,\beta}{D}$ becomes

$$8 \times 100 \times \cdot012 = 9\cdot6.$$
$$8 \times 30 \times \cdot012 = 2\cdot880.$$

Collecting these terms we have :—

1st term	$\left(\dfrac{1}{m}-1\right)^2$	$=$	1·85	1·85.
2nd ,,	$\left(\dfrac{A}{m'A'}-1\right)^2$	$=$	1	81
3rd ,,	$\left(\dfrac{1}{m''}-1\right)^2 \times 8 =$		1·48	1·48.
4th ,,	$\left(1-\dfrac{A}{0}\right)^2$	$=$	·25	·25.
5th ,,	$\left(\dfrac{A}{m_1 A_1}\right)^2$	$=$	2·25	2·25.
6th ,,	$\dfrac{2\,S\,L\,\beta}{A}$	$=$	2·88	9·64.
			9·71	96·47.

When all these causes of loss of *vis viva*, or motive

force, are present in the same draught the principle of
vis viva applied to this circulation will give us the
following relation :—

$$M V_1^2 + M\left(\frac{1}{m} - 1\right)^2 V^2 + M\left(\frac{A}{m'A'} - 1\right)^2 V^2 + M\left(\frac{1}{m''} - 1\right)^2 V^2$$
$$+ M\left(1 - \frac{A}{0}\right) V = 2(D - d) A H V - \frac{2 d S L \beta V^2}{g}.$$

In this general equation, the mass of air which passes
each section in one second is the same, and in the expression of its value

$$M = \frac{d A V}{g}$$

whence

$$\frac{d V}{g} = \frac{M}{A.}$$

Also according to the notation already employed

$$V_1 = \frac{A}{m_1 A_1} V$$

dividing both sides of the general equation by

$$M = \frac{d A V}{g}$$

we have the following,

$$V^2\left\{\left(\frac{A}{m_1 A_1}\right)^2 + \left(\frac{1}{m} - 1\right)^2 + \left(\frac{A}{m'A'} - 1\right)^2 + \left(\frac{1}{m''} - 1\right)^2 + \left(1 - \frac{A}{0}\right)^2\right.$$
$$\left. + \frac{2 S L \beta}{A} \right\}$$
$$= 2 g\left(\frac{D - d}{d}\right) H = 2 g \frac{a(t - T)H}{1 + a T}$$

whence

$$V = \sqrt{\frac{2 g\left(\frac{D - d}{d}\right) H}{\left(\frac{A}{m_1 A_1}\right)^2 + \left(\frac{1}{m} - 1\right)^2 + \left(\frac{A}{m'A'} - 1\right)^2 + \left(\frac{1}{m''} - 1\right)^2 + \left(1 - \frac{A}{0}\right)^2 + \frac{2 S L \beta}{A.}}}$$

or

$$V = \sqrt{\dfrac{2\,g\,\dfrac{a\,(t-T)\,H}{1+a\,T}}{\left(\dfrac{A}{m_1\,A_1}\right)^2 + \left(\dfrac{1}{m}-1\right)^2 + \left(\dfrac{A}{m'\,A'}-1\right)^2 + \left(\dfrac{1}{m''}-1\right)^2 + \left(1-\dfrac{A}{0}\right)^2 + \dfrac{2\,S\,L\,\beta}{A.}}}$$

Substituting for the denominator in this equation the values found for each term we have for the first

$$V = \sqrt{\dfrac{2\,g\left(\dfrac{D-d}{d}\right)H}{9\cdot71}} = 0\cdot3\sqrt{2g\left(\dfrac{D-d}{d}\right)H}\;;$$

and for the second value,

$$V = 0\cdot102\sqrt{2g\left(\dfrac{D-d}{d}\right)H}.$$

From the results of observation and experience it may be safely considered that the velocity as a rule lies between those given by using the two co-efficients 0·1 and 0·3. For ordinary practice, where there are not many very small tubes or very restricted passages over the bridge and elsewhere, and where the fire is not very thick and solid the co-efficient 0·3 may be used. Then

$$V = \cdot3\sqrt{2g\left(\dfrac{D-d}{d}\right)H}$$

$$V = 2\cdot4\sqrt{\dfrac{D-d}{d}H}.$$

In practice with a strong draught $\sqrt{\dfrac{D-d}{d}}$ differs very slightly from unity and may be left out, whence we have

$$V = 2\cdot4\sqrt{H}.$$

In using the correct formula $V \sqrt{\frac{D-d}{D}} H \times \frac{D}{d}$
we should have found that for the conditions of density, &c., usually found with boiler chimneys that
$\sqrt{\frac{D-d}{D}} \times \frac{D}{d}$ is usually about 1·4 where $\sqrt{\frac{D-d}{d}} = 1$,
whence we should have $V = 1·7 \sqrt{\frac{D-d}{D}} \times \frac{D}{d}$.

Where the length of the horizontal flues is great compared with that of the chimney and their diameter small, the velocity will be somewhat diminished.

With respect to the expression

$$\frac{D-d}{d} = a\left(\frac{t-T}{1+aT}\right)$$

Morin states that Peclet, in his "Traité de la Chaleur," 3rd ed., (p. 37, vol. i.,) has admitted

$$\frac{D-d}{d} = a\frac{(t-T)}{1+at}$$

an error which in many cases may materially alter the results, since the temperature T of the atmosphere scarcely ever varies more in this country than from 10° to 80°, making the denominator $1 + aT$, vary from 1·02 to 1·16, whilst the other denominator, $1 + at$, would vary from 1·2 to 2·3, and lead to very material mistakes. This, however, does not apply practically to boiler chimney draughts.

In the above mode of investigating the motive force of the draught it would have been more correct to have taken the *vis viva* of the cold air entering the ash-pit and fire-bars at the velocity due to its density, and to have made allowance for the change in the density as the air passed through the fire. It may be here remarked that theoretical and scientific refinements are unnecessary and often worse than useless in seeking to determine the actual velocity of the draught of any given chimney, when the circumstances and conditions are so complex and uncertain in actual practice that no theoretical formulæ can be expected to give results even approximately correct under all circumstances and conditions of working, which are continually varying. It is needless to seek to determine the exact pressures or densities at the top and bottom of the chimney in order to arrive at the average pressure and density at a given barometrical pressure when this pressure varies from day to day. The direction of the wind has a very decided effect upon the draught; when it blows strongly into the ash-pit and furnace it may greatly increase, and when it blows from the ash-pit it may greatly lessen, the motive force of the preponderating column of cold air. Then the shape of the chimney top, hygrometric condition of the atmosphere, presence of blow-holes or leakages in brickwork, angle or inclination to each other of bends at converging flues and points of uniting of split draughts, partial choking up of air passages and flues by clinkers, soot, and flue dirt, change in the quality of fuel, and many other uncertain circumstances likely to influence the force of the draught, are more important than smoothness of brickwork and any accurate determination of mean temperatures and densities. It is, however, well to know that uncertain conditions do exist, in order that we may know pretty nearly how far we may be guided by any rules we may find or establish for our own use.

In examining the general equation (pp. 7 and 13) we gather from the numerator with certainty :—

1st. That the velocity of the air and gases is proportionate to the square root of the height of the chimney, so that by doubling the height the theoretical velocity is increased only in the proportion of $\sqrt{1}$ to $\sqrt{2}$, or as 1 to 1·4, and in seeking to increase the draught by altering the height of the chimney we must quadruple the height in order to double the force of the draught, assuming that the area remains the same and that the additional height causes no more friction, which is, however, not the case, as the increase of height increases the value of the last terms in the denominator, in the equation in p. 7. In practice there is a limit to the height for the best draught, beyond which the additional height increases the resistance due to the increased velocity and friction more rapidly than the flow of cold air. For chimneys not over 3' 6" diam. at top this maximum height appears to be about 300ft.

2nd. That the velocity of the flow of cold air is proportionate to the square root of the ratio $\dfrac{D-d}{D}$. On examining this expression we find that the draught does not increase so quickly as the square root of the difference in temperature between the hot gases and the outside air, and that very little is gained theoretically by increasing the temperature of the gases in the chimney, when the ratio of the densities of the outside air and the hot gas are as 2 to 1. By raising the temperature from 600° to 1200° we should theoretically only increase the draught force in the proportion of ·71 to ·86, and in practice it would be still less.

On the other hand, when we place an economiser in

c

the flue and seek to reduce the temperature of the escaping gases from say 650° to 350°, we should diminish the velocity of the draught only in the proportion of $\sqrt{\cdot 75}$ to $\sqrt{\cdot 61}$, or as 1 is to 0·8.

3rd. From the denominator we gather that the velocity is inversely proportionate to the square root of a denominator in which at least six uncertain elements may combine to make its value equal to from 9 to 100, and, as the co-efficient of reduction depends in each case upon given conditions, the particular values should be introduced into the denominator.

The loss from these causes may be obviated

a, by facilitating the entrance of the air into the ash-pit and through the fire-bars and body of fuel, which may be done by making the dimensions of the passages as large as practicable, and making their shape as favourable as possible for the passage of air.

b, by avoiding as much as possible contractions, elbows, sudden bends, and alterations in the direction of the flow of air. Where contractions necessarily occur, there should be no corners left, but the contraction should be approached gradually by tapering the flue.

c, by avoiding as much as possible all enlargements, and especially sudden enlargements, in the flues, which cause eddies in the current of gases. Here again the flue should be tapered.

d, by making the surface of the masonry as smooth as possible.

e, by having no holes in the brickwork for the cold air to enter. Defects in the brickwork between two parts of a flue, by allowing the hot gases to make a shorter circuit to the chimney, will improve the draught at a sacrifice of economy, as the defective brickwork beneath the boiler practically reduces the extent of heating surface.

In estimating the volume of the gases of combustion, we can take the volume of the mixed carbonic acid, nitrogen, and unburnt oxygen, in the chimney, as equal to the original volume of air, and the density is increased simply in the ratio of the sum of the weights of the air and of the carbon taken up, to the weight of air. The volume of the mixed steam, nitrogen, and unburnt oxygen, is greater than the original volume of air by an amount equal to the quantity of oxygen that has combined with hydrogen, but the quantity of hydrogen in ordinary fuel bears so small a proportion to the total weight of fuel that it is not worth considering, and the volume of the gases in the chimney may be taken as equal to the volume of air at the given temperature.

Then the variation of density produced by the deviation of pressure from the mean atmospheric pressure may be disregarded.

The volume of the gas at 62^- and at one atmosphere may be taken as being sufficiently near for all practical purposes at 13 cubic feet for each lb. of air supplied to the furnace.

It has been shown in the author's "Treatise on Steam Boilers," p. 254, that a larger quantity of air than the theoretical amount for combustion passes the furnace, and the following are approximately the quantities of air required under different circumstances.

		Vol. of air at 62° per lb. of fuel.
12 lbs. per lb. of fuel	=	158
18 ,, ,,	=	236
21 ,, ,,	=	275
24 ,, ,,	=	306

The volume Q at any other temperature, t, may be found by the formula.

$$Q = Q_1 \frac{(461 + t)}{523}$$

Q_1 being the volume at 62°.

SUPPLY OF AIR IN LBS. PER LB. OF FUEL.

Temperature.	12	18	21	24
	Volume of gases per lb. of fuel in cubic feet.			
32°	148	222	259	297
62°	158	236	275	316
75°	162	242	282	324
98°	169	252	294	338
212°	204	304	355	408
300°	230	343	400	460
400°	260	388	452	5°0
500°	290	433	505	580
600°	320	480	558	640
700°	350	524	610	700
800°	380	570	663	760
1200°	500	748	871	1002
2000°	742	1109	1292	1485
2500°	894	1336	1556	1789
3000°	1044	1569	1818	2089
4000°	1346	2011	2343	2692

Let W = the weight in lb of fuel burnt *per second*.

Q_1 = volume at 62° of air supplied per lb. of fuel (see table).

A = sectional area of chimney in square feet.

Then V the velocity per second of the current in the chimney will be

$$V = \frac{W Q (461·2 + t)}{A \times 523}$$

$$W = \frac{V A \times 523}{Q (461 + t)}.$$

From this the weight of fuel per hour that can be burnt in the furnace can be calculated when we have found the velocity, V, by formula

$$V = 2·4 \sqrt{H}$$

The density, d, of the current in lb. per cubic feet is approximately

$$d = \frac{523}{461 + t} \cdot 0761 + \frac{1}{Q} ;$$

that is, from $0 \cdot 079 \left(\frac{523}{461 + t} \right)$ to $0 \cdot 082 \left(\frac{523}{461 + t} \right)$.

The head, H_1 expressed in feet, of a column of the outside air, may be converted into P_1, an equivalent pressure in lbs. per square foot thus —

$$P_1 = H_1 D = H_1 \times \cdot 0761,$$

the temperature of the atmosphere being taken at 62°. The unit of head most commonly employed is an inch of water, when syphon water gauges graduated into inches and decimals are used to measure the difference of pressure within and without the shaft. As a cubic foot of water at 62° weighs 62·355 lbs., a column of water one inch high must exert a pressure of 5·2 lbs. per square foot of surface, whence we have $\frac{1}{5 \cdot 2} = 0 \cdot 192$ for a multiplier, and Head in inches of water $= 0 \cdot 192 \, P_1 = H_0$

$$H_0 = 0 \cdot 192 \, H_1 \times \cdot 0761$$

and

$$H_1 = \frac{\text{Head in inches of water}}{\cdot 192 \times \cdot 0761} ;$$

from which formula we can calculate the height of chimney to give any required head, expressed in inches of water, when the temperature inside and outside are known :—Since $(p \, 4) \, H = \dfrac{H_1}{\dfrac{t'}{323 \times t'}}$ we have

$$H = \frac{\text{Head in inches of water}}{\cdot 192 \times \cdot 0761} \times \frac{523 \times t_1.}{t_1}$$

Suppose we want a chimney sufficiently high to give a head of $\frac{3}{4}$ inch of water, with the temperature inside at 523° above the temperature of the atmosphere we have then

$$H = \frac{\cdot 75}{\cdot 192 \times \cdot 0761} \times \frac{1}{\frac{t^1}{523 \times t_1}} = 103 \text{ feet.}$$

In the expression in Morin's formula for V the velocity of the air which passes up the chimney, it is obvious that this quantity increases indefinitely with the temperature T in the chimney, and it might appear that any increase in the temperature of the hot air would be attended with advantage for increasing the draught. It is not, however, the volume of air, or gases discharged by the chimney that it is desirable to increase, but rather that of the air passing through the grate. Now if we call this volume of the outside air Q_1, and its density D, the weight of air passing through the bars being equal to the weight of that discharged by the chimney, less the amount due to the weight of fuel burnt we have the relation

$$d\,Q = D\,Q_1,$$

whence

$$Q_1 = \frac{d\,Q}{D} = \cdot 95 \frac{1 + a\,T}{1 + a\,t} Q = \cdot 95 \frac{461 + T}{461 + t} Q.$$

Consequently Morin's formula for the volume Q at the temperature t would take the form

$$Q_1 = \frac{d}{D} A \sqrt{2\,G\,H\,\frac{t - T}{461 + T}} \cdot 95$$

$$= A \sqrt{2\,G\,H\,(461 + T)} \sqrt{\cdot 9 \frac{t - T}{(461 + t)^2}}$$

It is evident from this last form that whilst the weight of air to be discharged increases inversely as the temperature, the draught-force increases as the square root of the temperature, hence the weight of air Q_1 at the temperature T has a maximum value corresponding to a certain temperature t of the gas which is discharged from the chimney, and which should not be exceeded This is found from the factor

$$\sqrt{\frac{-T}{(461+t)^2}}$$

which expression attains a maximum when

$$t = \frac{461 + 2T}{\cdot 9}.$$

Therefore according to this theory of draught of Morin the best chimney draught takes place when the absolute temperature of the hot gas in the chimney is to that of the external air as $2\frac{1}{7}$ to 1 approximately, or when the head in hot gas $h = H$; that is, when the density of the hot gas is about one-half that of the external air. When the external temperature $T = 62°$ we have for the temperature within the chimney $\frac{461 \times 124}{\cdot 9} = 650$.

Although this result would be modified by taking into account the resistance to the flow of the gases in the long flue between a boiler furnace and the chimney, yet according to this theory, the temperature within any chimney to ensure the best draught should not much exceed 600°, and this limit is completely independent of any disparity in area of flues and chimney, and it is somewhat remarkable that the mean temperature of good boiler chimneys agrees pretty closely with this maximum temperature.

The proper allowance of air for a good chimney draught being about 21lbs. per lb. of fuel, the volume at 62° is about 275 cubic feet per lb. of fuel, and the volume of the hot gas at 600° about 558 cubic feet per lb. of fuel, or 27 cubic feet per lb. of the hot gas itself.

With respect to the head and temperature of the hot gas for the most effective draught, Rankine arrives at a similar result to the above as follows :—the velocity of the gas in the chimney is proportional to $\sqrt{h}$, and therefore to $\sqrt{0.96\{461+t-(461+T.)\}}$ The density of that gas is proportional to $\dfrac{1}{461+t}$.

The weight discharged per second is proportional to velocity × density, and, therefore, to $\dfrac{\sqrt{0.96\{461+t-(461+T)\}}}{461+t}$; which expression becomes a maximum, when

$$461 + t = \frac{2(461 + T)}{.96} = 2\tfrac{1}{12}(461 + T) ;$$

therefore the best chimney-draught takes place when the absolute temperature of the gas in the chimney is to that of the external air as 25 to 12.

Morin, in his "Étude sur la Ventilation," treats the hot air in the chimney as not having passed through the fire-bars, which is correct for some modes of ventilation, but not for boiler chimney-draught. He consequently gets the result equivalent to $t = 461 + 2T$, and remarks that Péclet, in the second edition of his Treatise, undertook an investigation for the temperature corresponding to the maximum of the volume of air drawn in by the chimney, and he arrived at the result just given, but the formulæ, which in the third edition of the same work are substituted for those in the second, being inaccurate, led him to suppress the investigation and its consequences, of which there is no longer question, in the third edition.

In what appears to be the correct theory of draught, where $V = \sqrt{2\,G\,H\left(a\dfrac{t-T}{1+at}\right)} \times \dfrac{461+t}{523}$, there is no such theoretical maximum temperature for the best draught, as above found by Rankine and Morin, since the velocity and volume of the flow of air increase continually with the increase of temperature t. According to the above expression, based on this theory, as the temperature increases, $\dfrac{a(t-T)}{1+at}$ approaches nearer and nearer to unity, and if we take the temperature $t = 200$ to $t = \infty$, we shall have the velocity of the cold air varying in the ratio of ·44 to 1, or as 1 to 2·3. As we have already seen at p. 17, when the density of the hot gas is about half that of the density of the outside air, or about 600°, the velocity has ·71 of the theoretical maximum. In practice, however, as the velocity and volume of the gases discharged increase with the rise of temperature, the resistance due to friction increases very rapidly also, and there is a maximum efficiency of draught which is not given by the formula. For boiler furnaces there is no practical gain in the draught, but a great waste of fuel by increasing the temperature of the escaping gases much beyond 600°.

In formula (p. 20) we had

$$W = \frac{V\,A \times 523}{Q\,(461+t)},$$

whence

$$A = \frac{W\,Q\,(461+t)}{V\,523},$$

taking the temperature of the discharged gases as 600° and 21 lbs. of air, per lbs. of fuel burnt $\dfrac{Q\,(461+t)}{523}$ becomes 558, and

$$A = \frac{W \times 558}{2 \cdot 4 \sqrt{H}}.$$

W is here the weight of coal burnt per second, but taking w as the weight burnt per hour, we have

$$A = \frac{w \times 0 \cdot 07}{\sqrt{H}}.$$

$$w = \frac{A \sqrt{H}}{0 \cdot 07}$$

$$H = \left(\frac{w \times 0 \cdot 07}{A} \right)^2$$

from which we have the column in the table for the area of a chimney to burn a given quantity of coal when the height is given in feet. The area in feet here is taken as that for the top opening of the chimney, and a conical or pyramidal chimney may be treated as though it were cylindrical or parallel. This agrees very nearly with the formulæ commonly given for land chimneys, and answers very well for a single boiler chimney, giving about $2\frac{3}{4}$ square feet for a Lancashire boiler consuming 10 tons of coal per week of 60 hours with a shaft 90 feet high.

Ninety feet is a very common height for boiler chimneys in large towns, being the minimum height allowed by many Town Improvement Acts, as in Manchester, Leeds, and other towns.

When, however, a number of boilers have only one chimney in common, the area does not require to be so large as the sum of several chimneys used for single boilers, since the friction becomes reduced, and the draught is greatly steadied when several boilers are fired successively, and a higher temperature is maintained.

The flues should be made larger than the area of the chimney, as they become contracted when soot and flue dirt gathers.

A common rule arrived at from experience is to make the flues and area of the chimney top equal to from $\frac{1}{8}$th to $\frac{1}{10}$th the area of firegrate without taking into account the height of the chimney. Another useful rule is to allow from 2 to 3 square feet for each boiler, having about 30 square feet of firegrate, the former allowance answering for chimneys over 150 feet high, which discharge the gases from several furnaces working together, and the latter for chimneys under 150 feet high, with not over six furnaces. There are many tall chimneys— over 200 feet—answering well with only from $1\frac{1}{4}$ feet to $1\frac{3}{4}$ feet square of top opening for every 30 square feet of firegrate where more than half-a-dozen boilers are working together with one chimney in common. It may be taken for granted that ordinary chimneys cannot be too high for obtaining a good draught.

It is usually considered that the larger the area of the chimney the better the draught, but this is not always the case with lofty chimneys where the gases can *cool down too rapidly* in a chimney of large section, and it has been found in several instances that when chimneys are very large for the number of boilers they serve, or for the quantity of coal burnt, as when a chimney is built to serve for future additions to the boiler power, the draught is improved by the better maintenance of temperature as additional boilers are set to work. When the area of the chimney is much larger than the aggregate area of the flues debouching into it, the diminution of friction and the expansion of the hot gases into a large area are favourable for the improvement of the draught. But the velocity of the ascent of the heated gases may be very much diminished, and in extreme cases, where the ascending current does not fill the chimney, so to speak, downward currents of air will be produced, especially with the wind in certain directions, to the impairment of the draught.

The effect of this may be seen in the lazy ascent of smoke from such chimneys, which are usually blackened at the top, and for some distance downwards. In a strong wind the smoke may be seen clinging to the leeward side of the chimney.

On the other hand, if the section be too small in proportion to the aggregate section of flues and fire-grate, the loss of force will be considerable, and can only be slightly increased by increasing the temperature of the escaping gases, which, as a rule, will be adverse to economical fuel consumption.

In practice it is found that with a lower pressure than half an inch of water it is difficult to keep a good fire without continual stirring, which is very wasteful, and produces smoke.

There can be no doubt that in still weather the height of the column of hot gas exceeds that of the chimney when the current of gases ascends beyond the summit, and with certain winds, when the shape of chimney top is favourable, the current of air will tend in many cases to increase the draught beyond that measured by the height of chimney. On the other hand, the shape of chimney-top may be such that the draft may be diminished in high winds, unless the wind blows direct into the ash-pit.

It is also known by experience that with certain states of the atmosphere, although the water-gauge may show a good draught, the fires do not burn briskly, in spite of the quantity of air with which they are supplied. The air appears to be comparatively dead when it blows, especially in the summer, and when it has prevailed from the south. It is not easy to account for this. The direction of the wind is not always a guide, nor indeed can it be expected to be, since it blows in whirls, and may be a south wind in one part of the island and a north wind in another part; yet it is certainly not a characteristic north wind that is found to affect the fires adversely.

The temperature of the escaping gases is usually ascertained by attaching small pieces of the following metals about 1″ long and ¼ inch square to a wire, and introducing them at any desired point in the flues or chimney, the time required to melt them being noted. The melting point of zinc is 700° Fahr.; of lead, 630°; bismuth, 493°; and of tin, 426°. When introduced into the flue behind the damper of Cornish and Lancashire boilers of moderate draught, it has been found that tin melts almost immediately, bismuth in about a minute; lead melts after a short time when the fires are clear, but zinc does not melt under any circumstances. It may therefore be assumed that 600°, or about the melting point of lead, is the average temperature of the escaping gases when the boilers are at work. This shows that the loss of heat is very considerable, and it may be approximately calculated as follows :—Taking the quantity of air used as about 21 lbs. per lb. of fuel, we have (see p. 253 of "Treatise") the weight of the products of combustion of 1 lb. of coal multiplied by the specific heat of the mixed gases $= 3.053$, and the remaining 9 lbs. of air multiplied by its specific heat $.238 = 2.142$. Adding these two products together, we have 5.195, and multiplying 293°, or the elevation of the temperature of the gases above the

boiler at 60 lbs. pressure, we have 15320 units of heat,
equivalent to 1·5 lbs. of water evaporated per lb. of
fuel, or taking the total heat of combustion at 2750°
the loss is equal to 10 per cent. compared with the
result that would be obtained if the hot gases escaped
at the temperature of the boiler.

In the table facing the title-page the sizes of chimneys
and flues required for various consumptions of fuel and
sizes of boilers are given. In the second column we have
the number of lbs. of coal per hour for the consumption
of which a chimney of given height and area is suitable.
Suppose we have two boilers, each having 35 sq. ft. of
grate area, burning 12 lbs. of coal per sq. foot of grate
per hour, equal to 840 lbs. of coal per hour, then, by
column 2 a chimney 90 feet high should have the
area at smallest part about $840 \div 135 = 6$ sq. feet,
that is, about 2 ft. 6 in. square, or 2 ft. 9 in. diam. In
columns 4, 5, 6 and 7 the horse-power of different areas
of chimney, and the areas for different horse-powers are
given. The somewhat meaningless term, horse-power,
as usually applied to chimneys, is here reluctantly
adopted in deference to the practice which still appears
likely to survive a long time in this country, of estimating the capability of boilers by their horse-power.

CHAPTER II.

WHEN the proper height and size of chimney have been decided upon to ensure a sufficient draught for the furnace, and also to satisfy the sanitary requirements of the case, the designing with respect to ornamentation, beauty of outline, and harmonising with surrounding buildings, belongs to the architect rather than to the engineer; but the design, so far as the stability of the structure is concerned, still lies within the engineer's province. The principles of stability have been laid down by Professor Rankine, who, up to the time of his death, was regarded as the first authority on this subject.

In estimating the safety and stability of a tall chimney shaft, the strains to be considered are—1st, the pressure exerted by the weight of the masonry or brickwork; and 2nd, the lateral pressure of the wind.

In order to resist the former strain, the best form of structure is that which gives an equal pressure per square unit of area in every section or "bed-joint." Taking, for simplicity, a solid cylinder, the weight evidently increases from the top downwards. This increase of weight must therefore be provided for by an increase in the sectional area as we descend. But this very increase of area augments the rapidity of growth of the mass as we descend, and the sectional area below must be further increased in consequence. For a structure whose centre of figure is the same as its centre of pressure, this law of increase may be deduced with the aid of the differential calculus as follows :—

Let W = weight of top layer of chimney,

  A = area of top section,

  k = coefficient of safety (for brick say 10 tons per square foot),

  c = weight of cubic foot of brickwork,

  a = any given section at distance h from the top,

  e = basis of natural logs = 2·71828 ;

then $W = A k$ or $A = \dfrac{W}{k}$, which gives us the first sectional area from the top to resist crushing. Any other section can be found by the formula

$$a = A\,e^{\frac{c}{k}h.}$$

$$\text{or } \log a = \log A + 0\cdot4343\,\frac{c}{k}h.$$

This formula applies also to hollow cylinders or cones having a straight batter inside.

It is evident from this formula that the outline of the structure will be a logarithmic line, practically straight at the top, and increasing in concavity as it approaches the bottom, giving what is called a "hollow batter." For ordinary chimneys 100 ft. high the amount of concavity required is not worth considering. For tall shafts, 300 ft. high and over, it is sometimes used. There is, however, this great advantage in using a straight batter instead of the theoretically correct hollow batter ; viz., the accuracy of the construction can be detected at any stage at a glance of the eye without the aid of instruments. Yet it must be conceded that the hollow batter is much more shapely, and may be worth the extra expense of building.

In a chimney made of blocks of stone or brick separated by plain joints, where there is no lateral pressure, the conditions of stability are—1st, that no joint shall be inclined to the horizon at a greater angle than that of repose, which in this case may be taken at $36\frac{1}{2}°$; and 2nd, that in any given bed-joint the centre of downward pressure, or point which is vertically below the centre of gravity of the superincumbent mass, shall not depart from the centre of figure of the joint more than a certain distance, which for round chimneys may be taken at $\frac{1}{4}$ the diameter of the joint, and for square chimneys $\frac{1}{3}$ the length of the joint.

In order to be able to calculate the strains caused by the lateral pressure of the wind, we must first consider the manner in which the chimney will fail by this pressure.

If the joints between the blocks of the material composing the structure had any tenacity such as the riveted or bolted joints of wrought or cast-iron, or of brick or stone held together by wrought-iron cramps, or by cement of a strength equal to that of the material it joins, the structure should be considered as one piece, and its strength determined by an investigation based on the theory of the strength of materials. But chimneys are usually made of brick or stone, the blocks of which, laid in mortar, touch each other at their joints, which are flat surfaces, held together by pressure and friction, but *not by tension*, so long as the mortar is fresh, and on this basis the stability ought to be considered. Even a year after mixture, the strength of good mortar is only about 50 lbs. per square inch, and

D

a large proportion of failures of chimneys have occurred
before the mortar has had time to set, which shows
that the strength of the mortar should never be taken
into account in designing a new chimney; but for old
chimneys the strength of the mortar may also be considered, and taken at 8000 lbs. per square foot when not
less than eighteen months old. In cases where chimneys
have been sawn to restore them to the perpendicular,
and the joints have not been properly remade with
mortar or cement, the weight of the chimney can alone
be depended upon for its stability.

In designing a new chimney, we may then disregard
the tenacity of the mortar, and consider the chimney
as being simply set upon its foundation and held down
only by its own weight, upon which alone it is dependent for its stability. The moment of stability for a new
chimney at any point is evidently half the diameter of
the bed-joint, B_1, at this point, × the weight, W, of the
chimney above this joint, or $W \times \dfrac{B}{2}$.

For an old chimney, if we make the solid area in
square feet at the joint $= B_1$, we have the moment of
stability $= (W + B_1 \times 8000) \dfrac{B}{2}$.

The lateral pressure of the wind may be assumed to
act horizontally, and to be of uniform intensity at all
heights above the ground. The greatest intensity in
this country, against a flat surface directly opposed to
it, used to be taken by Rankine at 55 lbs. per square
foot, but in 1868 the pressure of the wind at Liverpool was registered at nearly 80 lbs. per square foot, the
highest ever known in this country. For new chimneys
the pressure of the wind may still be taken at 55 lbs.

The inclination of the surfaces due to the batter or slope of the chimney is usually not sufficient to be taken into account in estimating the pressure of the wind against it.

A circular chimney may be considered as cylindrical in plan, and the total effect of the pressure against the side of a cylinder may be taken as being equal to one-half the total pressure against its diametral plan, or against the side of a square chimney of equal diameter, which for the strongest winds gives us 40 lbs. per square foot. This result is arrived at thus: Let $AB = p$, the force of the wind (in fig. 2) in a direction parallel to the diameter, XY, of the chimney. Resolving AB into its component parts at right angles, and with one of

Fig. 2.

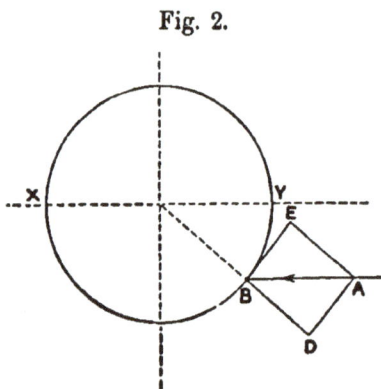

them, BD, as a normal to the curve at the point B, we have BD as the measure of force exerting pressure towards the centre of the chimney, and $BD = p$ sin $\angle ABD$. We have now to resolve this force again to get the component as measuring the effective pressure in a direction parallel with that of the wind, whence we have p sin$^2 \angle ABD$. Taking a number of points affected by the wind, the mean sine of the arcs will be about ·75. The square of ·75 = ·56, whence the mean effective pressure on the semicircumference $= p$ ·56.

If the pressure on a square chimney be taken		=	1·
that on an Hexagonal chimney may be taken		=	0·75
,, Octagonal ,, ,,		=	0·65
,, Circular ,, ,,		=	0·5

Let S = the area in square feet of the vertical section through the middle of the portion of the chimney above the base or joint B C (fig. 3), then for a square chimney the total pressure P against the side $= p\,S$, and for a round and octagonal chimney $P = p\dfrac{S}{2}$. The resultant of this pressure may be considered to act in a horizontal line

Fig. 3.

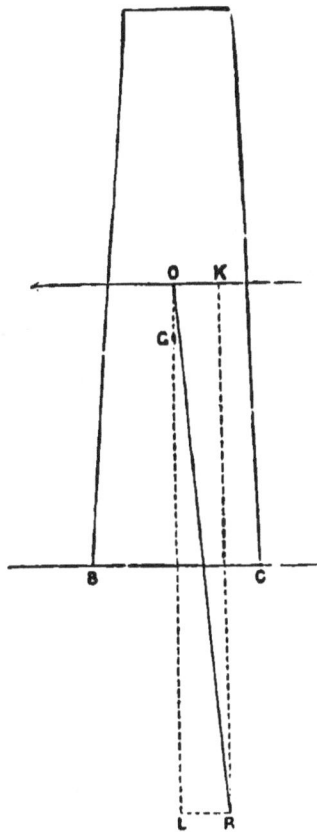

through O, the centre of gravity of the vertical diametral section. This centre of gravity may be found thus : let A B C D in fig. 4 represent the vertical section of a chimney or division of a chimney. Draw the diagonals B C and A D. On C B mark off C E = O B, and bisect A D in F. Join E F, then the point where E F cuts the centre line of the figure is the centre of gravity. Let H = the height of this centre O above the joint B C in fig. 3, then the moment of pressure is H P $=$ H p S for a square chimney, and $H\ P\ =\ \dfrac{H\ p\ S}{2}$ for a round or octagonal chimney, and to this moment of pressure " *the least moment of stability* " of the portion of the chimney above the joint or base B C should be equal. A balance of moments will exist when $H P = W\dfrac{B}{2}$, in the case of a new chimney, or $H P = (W + B_1 \times 8000) \dfrac{B}{2}$

for an old chimney. To ensure stability, it is evident the moment of stability must exceed the overturning moment. In practice a factor of safety of 2 is sufficient to use, whence we have $H P \times 2 = W \dfrac{B}{2}$, or $(W + B_1 \times 8000) \dfrac{B}{2}$.

It is advisable to describe these forces graphically, as in fig. 3. Draw the vertical line O G L through the centre of gravity G of the chimney, or of the division above the joint in question, as may be required. Let O be the centre of pressure against the side. Set off O K equal to P and O L = W. Complete the parallelogram, and join O R then when the line O R crosses the base or joint B C at a distance of $\frac{1}{4}$ of B C from the centre O L, the chimney is sufficiently stable to prevent overturning.

Fig. 4.

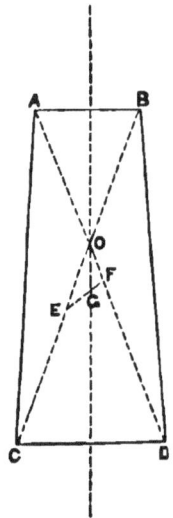

It may be considered that the lines of resistance in a square and circular shaft of the same height are very nearly identical in shape and position when the diameter and sides of the square are respectively equal. This is in consequence of the round chimney, although containing less material, being subject to less pressure.

The manner in which a chimney yields to the pressure of the wind is, however, by the opening or cracking of one of the bed joints at the windward side, without completely overturning. This opening gradu-

ally extends, in a more or less regular zig-zag course
diagonally downwards towards the lee side. The
complete destruction eventually takes place, either
by the shifting of the upper portion past its support
below, or by the crushing of the brick-work at the lee
side by the too great pressure concentrated there, or
in many cases, from both causes acting together, and
in all cases the upper portion of the chimney falls to
pieces inside and out, filling the interior of the portion
left standing.

The resistance to the horizontal shifting of a bed
joint, is due to the friction of the horizontal faces of
the blocks of stone or brick, and is called "frictional
tenacity," whose amount at any given joint is the product of the vertical load on the joint into the coefficient of friction, which for masonry and brick-work
with damp mortar, is about 0·74.

The tendency of the wind pressure being to open
the bed joint at the windward side, and to crush the
material at the leeward side, or to overturn the structure above the joint in a plane parallel with the
direction of the wind, it is evident that the centre of
resistance of the structure will be moved towards the
lee side.

It has been found by experience necessary to limit
this deviation of the centre of resistance from the centre
of figure, so that the maximum intensity of pressure
at the leeward edge shall not exceed twice the mean
intensity. Denoting by q the ratio which the distance
of this deviation bears to the diameter of the joint j,
we have

for round chimneys $q = \frac{1}{4}$ the dia. of the joint.
for square   „ $q = \frac{1}{6}$ „   „

The moment of stability of a chimney at any given bed joint is the product of the weight of the structure, or of the weight of the structure plus the tenacity of the mortar as the case may be, above that joint into the horizontal distance qj. If the axis of the chimney be vertical, as in fig. 3, the limiting distance $q\,j$, for the centre of pressure will be the same in all directions. But most chimneys are found to have their axes not quite vertical, and the least moment of stability is evidently that which resists the pressure in that direction towards which the axis of the chimney leans. In estimating the stability of existing chimneys this must be taken into account. In figure 5 let G be the centre of gravity of the structure above the joint $A\,B = j$, and let E be a point in the joint vertically below it, and let $q'\,j =$ the distance of the point E from the middle of the joint j, then the least moment of stability is denoted by $W \times E\,F = (q - q')\,Wj$, F being the limiting position of the centre of resistance of the joint, all dimensions being in feet, and p being taken at 55 lbs. for new chimneys.

Fig. 5.

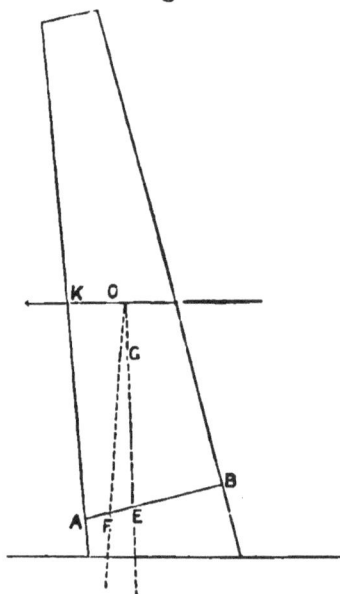

Then for round chimneys.

$$\frac{h\,p\,S}{2} - \left(\frac{1}{4} - q'\right) W\,j.$$

and for square chimneys

$$h\,p\,S = \left(\frac{1}{3} - q'\right) W\,j.$$

From these equations the following are deduced for practice. Let t = mean thickness of brickwork above the joint B C, w = the weight of 1 cubic foot of brickwork = 112 lbs. as a rule, d = mean outside diameter of chimney, then we have approximately—

For round chimneys, $W = 3\cdot14\ wt.\ \left(\dfrac{d-t}{d}\right)$ S.

For square chimneys, $W = 4\quad wt.\ \left(\dfrac{d-t}{d}\right)$ S.

substituting these values in the equations just given, we have the following formula which will be found useful:—

For round chimneys, $H\,p = (1\cdot57 - 6\cdot28\,q')\,wt.\ \left(\dfrac{d-t}{d}\right)j.$

For square chimneys, $H\,p = \left(\dfrac{4}{3} - 4\,q'\right)\,wt.\ \left(\dfrac{d-t}{d}\right)j.$

When we require to know the mean thickness of brickwork for a new chimney, the form and dimensions being given, we have the following tentative formulæ, the results being multiplied by $\dfrac{d}{d-t}$ for the actual thickness, when t is so found.

$$t = \frac{H\,p}{1\cdot57\ wj}\ \text{for round chimneys.}$$

$$t = \frac{H\,p}{\frac{4}{3}\,w\,j}\ \text{for square chimneys.}$$

The outside diameter of the chimney at the ground line should not, as a rule, be less than $\frac{1}{10}$th the height. The batter varies from 1 in 60 to 1 in 10 : 1 in 24 is very common.

A chimney shaft is made up of a series of steps or courses, one above the other. Each step is of uniform thickness, but as we ascend, each succeeding step is thinner than that which it rests upon, so that the bed joints between the steps, where the thickness changes, have less stability than the intermediate bed joints, and it is only these former to which it is necessary to apply the formulæ in determining the strength and stability of the structure.

The height of the different steps of uniform thickness varies greatly according to the judgment and practice of the architect or builder, and the custom in different districts.

If we take the safe load that can be borne by good brickwork, at 20,000 lbs. per square* foot, and the weight of brickwork with little mortar at the joints at 115 lbs. per cubic foot, we have $20,000 \div 115 = 170$, approximately, as the extreme height in feet, we should make any single division, or length, of uniform thickness. This length is very seldom approached even in the tallest shafts, as the brickwork has also to bear the weight due to force of wind acting against the opposite side of chimney, in addition to the chimney itself. The steps, or courses, should not exceed 90 feet in height, except in cases where the chimney shaft is inside a tower which protects it from the wind. In chimneys from 90 to 120 ft. high, the lengths vary from 17 to 25 ft., the top height being 1 brick thick; in chimneys from 130 to 150 ft., the lengths are from 25 to 35 ft.; in chimneys from 150 to 200 ft. the lengths are from 35 to 50 ft. the top length being 1½ brick thick, and in very tall chimneys, that is, from 200 to 300 ft., and over, the lengths vary from 50 to 90 ft., the thickness of top length being 1½ bricks.

* As the crushing strength of ordinary brickwork is much less than 90 tons to the square foot, the strength of the bricks used in very high structures should be ascertained by experiment.

The binding of the masonry * is often increased by laying at intervals hoop-irons, tarred and sanded, in the bed joints, the ends being turned down into the side joints. The length of the hoop-iron in each joint, should be twice the circumference of the chimney at that part.

Forge chimneys are often strengthened by strong bands of wrought iron, placed at intervals outside; but these are not necessary for boiler chimneys. Sometimes strong hoops about $3'' \times \frac{1}{2}''$ are built in at intervals of 12 to 18 feet, to prevent cracks, but unless the chimney is provided with a very efficient lightning conductor, these masses of iron are apt to prove dangerous during a thunder-storm.

It is usual, and expedient, to protect the inside of the chimney with a lining of fire brick. For forge and ironworks' chimneys, where the gases escape at a very high temperature, the lining should be carried all the height. If care be taken to heat the chimney gradually for the first time of working, and subsequently, when it has been allowed to become cold, it is not necessary to have an air space between the firebrick lining and the shaft proper. In this case the lining may be included in the thickness of brickwork necessary for the strength and stability of the shaft. The firebrick lining may then be bonded into the other brickwork in the ordinary way, the thickness of the lining being $\frac{1}{2}$ brick in the upper portion, and 1 brick in the lower portion, and should be laid in fire clay, and not in mortar like the other brickwork.

* The bond usually adopted is 1 course of headers to 4 of stretchers. In circular chimneys a uniform bond for the outside course of brickwork is sometimes rec' lessly adopted.

In boiler chimneys it is, however, unnecessary to carry the lining all the way to the top. In small chimneys, under 100 feet high, it may be carried one-third, or one-half the way up, and in chimneys of great height, the lining need not be carried higher than from 50 to 80 feet, according to the height of the chimney shaft.

An arrangement often used, is to carry the lining up parallel, that is, without taper, and to let the outside shaft meet it at a very acute angle. This leaves an air space between the lining and the main body of the shaft, which should be provided with air holes, communicating with the external atmosphere, but carefully sealed from communication with the inside. This caution is necessary, because when the gases that pass through the flues have access to the air space round the lining, there is always a risk of damage being done by the explosion of inflammable mixtures of gas and air that may collect. It is, therefore, advisable, when an air space is provided, not to allow any communication between it and the inside flue, consequently the plan of leaving the air space open to flue at top, so often done, cannot be recommended.

It is, however, perhaps, best to dispense with the air space altogether, as the difference between the temperature of the portions of the chimney above and below the top of the air space, renders the masonry liable to fracture at this part, and many chimneys may be found so fractured without the actual cause being suspected.

In erecting a chimney, care should be taken that the building is not proceeded with too rapidly. It is sometimes restricted to a rate not exceeding 6 feet a day in height. It is advisable to build chimneys when the work can be most steadily proceeded with. When the structure is built up too rapidly, and the mortar has not time to set, a gale of wind is liable to press the chimney over to one side, where it stays—the compressible nature of the mortar offering little or no resistance. Consequently, the less mortar used the better. Cement, owing to its crumbling when exposed to a high temperature, cannot be recommended except for the top of the chimney, where it may, however, be usefully employed. Grouting should, as a rule, not be attempted.

In order to gain admission into flues and chimneys, many engineers and architects make doors in the sides or crown of the horizontal flues leading to the chimney. A much better plan, however, is to make an arched opening at the bottom of the chimney, or in the pedestal, at one side of, or opposite the flue entrance. This opening can be readily built up air tight. Such a provision in the chimney may be required for introducing a fire of wood and shavings, to cause the boiler fire to draw on first lighting up, after the flues have been allowed to become cold and damp, especially when they descend to the chimney. This opening would be of service when it is advisable to make experiments on the draught, which are too often overlooked, but which may be of great service in detecting a falling off in the draught, and lead to the detection of air leakages, and other defects that may operate strongly against the economical or efficient working of the boilers.

With respect to the best position for the dampers for regulating the draught, apart from all consideration of economy and efficiency, it is most convenient to have them at the end of the external flues of the boilers, or between the boiler and the chimney. The dampers are therefore generally so placed, but this is the least advantageous position for preserving the temperature in the flues and chimney, and the energy of the draught, which would be best preserved at meal-times and over night, by placing the damper on the top of the chimney. Here, however, it would not keep the flues under the boiler so warm as when placed in its usual position behind the boiler, and the effect would be felt in lighting up on Monday mornings.

Dampers at the ashpit might be used with some advantage in maintaining the temperature of the boiler flues.

The depth and area of the foundation will depend very much upon the nature of the ground upon which the chimney is built. In many cases where chimneys are built on the banks of a river, and other places where the upper strata are of alluvial clays, soft silts and made ground, it is necessary to go to a depth of 25 or 30 feet, or even more, to reach a good stiff clay, hard sand or rock. This depth below the surface is excavated and filled in with concrete in various ways, or piled, according to the practice of the locality, or judgment of the engineer, so as to economise material without risking unequal settling of the structure, which cannot be too carefully guarded against, as it has often led to the failure of the chimney.

CHAPTER III.

DESCRIPTIONS OF CHIMNEYS.

THE following account of some of the largest brick and stone chimneys that have been built may be of interest. The highest chimney is at Mr. Townshend's Works, Port Dundas, Glasgow; and it is, with the exception of the spire at Strasburg, the Great Pyramid, and the spire of St. Stephen's at Vienna, the loftiest building in the world. It is circular in section, and rises to a height of 454 feet from the ground. The foundations are laid 14 feet below the surface on a bed of stiff clay, mixed with pebbles, and consist first of six courses of hard brick on edge, covering a circular area of 47 feet in diameter, diminished by outward "scarcements" to a diameter of 44 ft. Over this solid substratum the foundation proper consists of twenty-six courses of brick also on edge, diminished by scarcements on both sides from 21′ 9″ to 8′ 6″ thick. At the surface the outside diameter is 32 ft., with walls 5′ 3″ thick (6½ bricks). There is an inside lining of firebrick carried up 50 feet, with an air space round it. At the cope the outside diameter is 12″ 8′, with 14 inch walls, the total height of the building being 468 feet. The thickness diminishes by half a brick every step. There are six steps; the first of 40 ft., then four of 80 ft., the top step being 94 ft. The outside batter is straight from bottom to top. The point of least stability is at top of second step from the ground.

In Glasgow there is also the celebrated chimney at the works of Messrs. Tennant and Co., St. Rollox. From the base of foundation to the top of chimney it measures 455½ feet. The section above ground consists of five steps,—54, 60, 96, 140 and 85 ft. in height. Commencing from the ground the thickness of wall at ground is four bricks; and diminishing half a brick at each step, being two bricks thick at top. The outside diameter at ground level is 40 feet, and at summit 13′ 6″. The point of least stability is at top of third step. The foundation is 50 feet square, and 20 feet deep. The inner chimney is a cylinder 16 feet diam., and 260 ft. high. It is not connected with the outer one, but nearly touches it at the top. The weight of the chimney is estimated to be about 7,000 tons.

In Halifax, at Messrs. Crossley's, Dean Clough Mills, there is a large octagonal chimney of stone. Its height when built was 381 feet, but some of the top was removed on account of the immense weight at the foundation. The width at the bottom is 30 ft. Nearly 10,000 tons of brick and stone were used in the erection, being considerably more than the weight of Messrs. Townshend's chimney in Glasgow.

The tall brick chimney at the Edinburgh Gas Works is 341½ feet from the bottom of the foundation. The shaft is circular, 264 feet high, and built in steps of 35, 40, 48, 58 and 83 ft., commencing from the base, which is 3½ bricks thick, the highest being 1½ bricks. The inside diameter of shaft is 20 ft. at base, and 11′ 4″ at top. The foundation and pedestal, which are square, are of stone, 77½ ft. high. The cost was nearly £5,000.

At Huddersfield there is a tall circular chimney at Messrs. Brooks's Fireclay Works. It measures from the foundation 321 ft., and rises 306 ft. clear above the ground. The base at the foundation is 36 ft. square. At the ground line it is 31 ft. and at the summit 11 ft. diameter. The flue is 14 ft. diam. at the bottom and 9 ft. at the top.

In Bradford, at Messrs. Mitchell Bros.' factory, there is an octagonal stone chimney, that rises 300 feet above the ground. The foundations consist of two courses of concrete 22 ft. and 21 ft. square by 12 inches thick each, resting upon the rock. It measures 20 ft. across at the foundation and 9 ft. at the summit.

At the West Cumberland Hæmatite Iron Works, there is a circular brick chimney, designed by Prof. Rankine, 251 feet above the ground, with 17 ft. foundation below. Inside diameter of basement is 18 ft. 10 in. Inside diameter of the four circular archways for flues, 7 ft. 6 in. Outside diameter at top of cone, 15 ft. 3 in., and 1½ brick thick; outside diam. at 2 ft. above bottom, 25 ft. 7 in.; outside diam. of square basement, 30 ft. × 30 ft.; outside dimensions of foundation course, 31 ft. 6 in.; outside dimensions of concrete, 34 ft. 6 in. sq. There are three steps, the two uppermost being 80 ft. each, whilst the bottom one is 88 ft. high. At summit the thickness is 1½ brick; at bottom of lowest step, 2 ft. above the ground, 2½ bricks, increasing by courses four bricks in order to spread the pressure. The cost was £1,560.

The well known chimney of the Shell Foundry at Woolwich Arsenal is 223 ft. 9 in. above the ground, with 16 ft. of brickwork below, making 239 ft. 9 in. above the bed of concrete. The base above the ground is 20 ft. square, with plinth and cornice, 27 ft. high, on which the octagonal shaft is erected. It is 16 ft. 9 in.

diam. at base, and 6 ft. 6 in. at top. The walls are 2 ft. 7½ in. thick at bottom of shaft, and are reduced by steps of 37½ ft. 4½ in., the top step of 26 ft. being 9 in. thick. The uppermost 9 ft. is bell-mouthed, and built in cement. The Portland stone cap weighs about 17 tons.

Perhaps the tallest *square* chimney in this country is that at the Camperdown Linen Works, near Dundee. This chimney, or rather tower, rises 282 feet from the ground. It is somewhat in the Italian style, and is built of variegated brick. At the summit of the tower, which is 230 ft. high, constructed in panels, there is a balcony, above which the shaft is octagonal. The thickness of the walls at the ground is 5 ft., at the balcony 2 ft. 6 in., and at the top 18 inches. This tower is quite distinct from the chimney proper, which is circular in form, 14 ft. 6 in. diam. at base, and 13 ft. 3 in. at top. Its thickness is 18 in. from ground to first panel; 14 in. from this to the balcony, and 9 in. from balcony to summit. The tower is 24 ft. 6 in. sq. at the ground, and 20 ft. sq. at the balcony, above which it tapers gradually to the summit. The weight is about 5,000 tons, and the cost is said to have been about £6,000.

At Messrs. Lister's, Manningham Mills, Bradford, there is a lofty square chimney, 249 ft. high, with panelled sides, and circular top. The inside of the square at ground is 10 ft., gradually increasing to 11 ft.

At Connah's Quay, Chester, there is another lofty square chimney, 245 feet high from the ground. The size inside is 17 ft. 6 in. at base, and 7 ft. at top. Its cost is said to have been but little over £2,000.

Besides the circular, octagonal, and square forms

generally used, there are a few peculiar shapes sometimes met with.

With a view to get a parallel flue from bottom to top
without using an inside shaft, the walls of a square
chimney may be carried up in one thickness about
150 ft. high, and 14 inches thick. In order to obtain
stability two buttresses are run up at each side, tapering
to nothing at the summit. There is a chimney of this
kind at the South Metropolitan Gas Works.

Some chimneys have been built, having a section
like an eight-pointed star, the inside being octagonal or
circular, with or without inside lining, or air space.

Iron chimneys are seldom used except for small boilers,
and are usually of small dimensions, and made circular.
A few, however, have been erected within the last ten
years of considerable dimensions. There are two at the
Creusot Works in France. One is 197 ft. high, 4 ft. 3 in.
dia. at top, and 10 ft. at bottom. It is constructed with
a hollow batter, and is firmly bolted to masonry work
just clear of the ground. It was riveted together
horizontally, and lifted into its place with a crane.
The thickness of the plates is $\frac{3}{32}$ in. at top, and $\frac{7}{16}$ in.
at bottom. Its weight is 28 tons.

There is a still larger chimney at Creusot, of which a
description will be found in " Engineering," vol. xiii.
It is 279 feet high, 7 ft. 6½ in. dia. at the top, 22 ft. 11½ in.
at the bottom, and weighs 80 tons. It is built also
with a hollow batter, and is held by bolts and a strong
angle-iron ring, to a mass of masonry weighing about
300 tons. Its cost was about £1,600.

The experience in such chimneys is not yet sufficient
to enable us to judge with any degree of certainty of
their durability. It is, however, certain that with some

kinds of fuel, in spite of careful painting and partial lining with brickwork, their destruction will be very rapid, and the adoption of iron chimneys can only be recommended where the cost of brick and stone precludes their adoption.

A brick or stone chimney, substantially built, and with a fair margin of stability, will last many generations, whilst an iron chimney of moderate thickness cannot be depended upon, in many cases, to last more than forty or fifty years.

THE SHAPE OF CHIMNEY TOPS.

Although the position and surroundings of the furnaces, with respect to the direction of the wind, have a very decided influence upon the draught, and may outweigh any small advantage that one chimney top may have over another, yet it must be admitted that the shape of the top has a perceptible influence in promoting or retarding the draught when a strong wind is blowing.

Some chimneys, which are not excessively wide, have a better draught in all high winds, which may be accounted for by the arrangement of the boiler-house, its surroundings producing a greater pressure of air at the furnaces when a gale is blowing. In some arrangements a gale from a certain quarter may have an exhausting action, tending to draw the air from the furnaces, whilst a gale from the opposite quarter tends to increase the pressure at the furnaces, and so improves the draught.

With a plain or "bluff" top, a strong wind may act partially as a damper, as may sometimes be seen by the action it has upon the column of smoke as it issues

from the chimney. The wind not only flattens the
escaping column, but it also tends to produce downward eddies, especially in very large chimneys. There
is often evidence of the downward eddies on the outside
in the blackened appearance of the masonry on the lee
side of the chimney. But as the wind, striking against
a bluff top tends to rise vertically in the first place, and
clear the windward side of the chimney at a short distance above it, this shape is decidedly better than that
of some of the tops so often seen, which are concave at
the rim and convex at the orifice, and appear to be
designed to guide the wind right into the chimney and
check the draught. A better shape for an open top is
concave towards the orifice, so as to give the wind an
upward direction, whereby the tendency will be rather
to promote than check the draught.

When there is both an inner and outer shaft, the
design for deflecting the current of air upwards can be
carried out to the greatest advantage. The top of the
inner shaft should be stopped off a few feet below that
of the outside shaft and surmounted by a concave
deflecting cap, from which the currents of air admitted
through suitable openings in the outer shaft are deflected
upwards and not only prevent any downward eddying,
but tend to induce an exhausting action in the inner
shaft, and consequently to promote the draught. At
the same time the top of the outside chimney should be
surmounted with a concave deflecting cap.

It appears strange that in the endless variety of
designs for chimney caps, in the case of a single shaft,
advantage has never or very seldom been taken of the
opportunity to make the cap hollow, and in such a
manner as to cause an induced current upwards on the

same principle as that just mentioned for a double shaft.

Some very shapely chimney caps are made concave below and convex above; were they made concave both above and below they would have the best form for splitting the current of wind, and so prevent it from interfering with the draught.

Covered tops of a pyramidal shape, having vertical, tapered openings at the corners, have been used with decided advantage. By this arrangement the wind can blow into only one or at most two of the openings at once, leaving the others free to discharge fully. The sum of the areas of the openings should in this case be considered as the size of the orifice of the chimney. When practicable, the openings should be so arranged that when the wind is blowing from the chimney to the furnaces, it does not tend to blow down any of the openings, or, in other words, one side of the top should face the furnaces when these are behind the chimney.

The cost of chimneys varies within very wide limits. A few years ago chimneys up to 90 feet high could be built in the Midland Counties in a certain style for £1 per foot, but a more usual cost is from £2 to £2 10s. per foot, for chimneys up to 100 feet high. As much as £22 a foot has been paid for some of the ornamental tall towers with inside shafts.

CHAPTER IV.

CHIMNEYS—LIGHTNING CONDUCTORS.

THERE are many engineers at the present time who argue that lightning conductors are useless, or even worse than useless ; hence the number of tall chimneys seen unprovided with lightning rods in various parts of the country.

The destructive effects of lightning are much more frequent and ruinous than is generally supposed. Whilst some twenty cases could be quoted where lightning has fallen on unprotected powder magazines, and caused their explosion, killing thousands of people, and laying whole towns in ruins, it may be questioned whether a single case can be cited of a powder magazine being struck, that was properly protected by a lightning conductor.

The causes of the widespread disbelief in conductors as a means of preserving chimneys and other lofty buildings against the destructive action of lightning, are :—

1. The opinion commonly held, and often where we should least expect to find it, viz., that metallic bodies, especially when pointed, *attract* lightning, and are therefore dangerous. This opinion is probably due to the fact that during thunderstorms luminous points have often been seen on spires, vanes, ship's masts, and other elevated metallic bodies. The glowing appearance here spoken of is unattended by any heating effects, and is harmless.

This phenomenon, like some other effects of atmospheric electricity, is due to the highly charged electrical condition of the clouds and atmosphere, and it is at once concluded that these bodies have a superior attractive force for electricity over all others. Now metallic bodies, whether pointed or not, have no more power of *attracting or drawing* the lightning to them than non-metallic bodies, and it is the confusing of the apparent with the actual attractive force, or erroneously concluding that metals are good attracters because they are good conductors, that has brought about the misunderstanding on this point. Now in no case can it be said that the conductor attracts the lightning in the active and adverse sense which is here implied, and in which this term is often used. On the other hand, the conductor acts, especially when its top is pointed, in preventing the prominence to which it is applied from becoming highly electrified *by induction*, and in so much actually prevents the structure from attracting the cloud that electrifies it. On an electrified cloud passing over a pointed conductor, the opposite and induced electricity of the earth is discharged from the point of the conductor, and the cloud and air are often thereby neutralised without producing lightning at all. But when a discharge does take place the duty of the conductor is entirely passive : by offering a line of comparatively small resistance, it determines the direction of the discharge, which is not, however, in the first place brought about by the presence of the conductor, or, what more often happens, the presence of the uninsulated pointed conductor, by its peculiar property, prepares the resisting air in such a manner that the current of electricity is discharged quietly and without violence or a flash of

lightning. Should, however, the electrified clouds be
driven to the erection by the winds in such masses that
the opposite kind of electricity does not stream away
from the point of the conductor in sufficient quantities
to prevent a spark from passing, the spark, or flash of
lightning, will pass from the cloud to the conductor in
preference to any neighbouring point, since the electric
density will be greater here, and the resistance least.
Hence the duty of the conductor may be considered as
being entirely passive, as, by offering a line of comparatively small resistance, it determines the direction of
the discharge when it becomes inevitable, although it
is not brought about by the presence of the conductor
in the first place, but by the action of the clouds and a
large area of ground. To use an oft repeated simile,
the conductor no more attracts the lightning than a
water-spout, on the side of a house, attracts the rain
from the clouds which it leads to the drain in the
ground.

The fact that so many well-known buildings, which
were repeatedly struck by lightning before being fur-
nished with rods, have escaped being struck after the
lightning rods were applied, would appear to be con-
clusive evidence of the passive character of the pointed
conductor with respect to the discharge, and that its
presence averts a violent explosion by rapidly neutralising the electrical condition of the atmosphere.

The luminous appearance, accompanied by a whiz-
zing noise, sometimes observed when a very dense discharge is received by the conductor, is of a perfectly
harmless character, and is probably of the same nature
as the "glow" discharge, so well known to those who
have made and witnessed electrical experiments.

2. The disbelief in the efficacy of lightning conductors is sometimes due to the carelessly expressed opinions of many writers on electricity, to the effect that thoroughly efficient lightning conductors might discharge the electricity *gradually* and harmlessly into the ground, but would be a poor protection to the building in the event of its being struck by a flash. Now, in answer to this, there are many cases on record of ships and buildings having been struck by lightning. Those provided with efficient conductors have borne the shock unharmed, whilst those unprotected have suffered severely. Perhaps the most convincing evidence of the efficiency of good lightning conductors is that adduced by Sir W. S. Harris from the journals of H. M. ships. In 1861, he writes, " We had between the years 1810 and 1815, that is, within about five years, no less than 40 sail of the line, 20 frigates and 12 sloops and corvettes, placed *hors de combat* by lightning. In 250 such cases, 100 seamen were killed and 250, at least, severely hurt. In the merchant navy, within a comparatively small number of years, no less than 34 ships, most of them large vessels, with valuable cargoes, have been totally destroyed, being either burnt or sunk, to say nothing of a host of vessels partially destroyed or severely damaged. Damage to H. M.'s ships by lightning has happily ceased (since effective conductors were applied); it is now not known in the British navy." Damage to ships by lightning seldom occurs now, as most ships are fitted with wire ropes, which act as lightning conductors.

3. A more reasonable objection, at first sight, to the use of conductors, is that many buildings have been damaged in spite of the presence of lightning rods,

and when it is assumed that a conductor acts by attracting the lightning, which would not take place but for the conductor's presence, the doubt at once arises whether the amount of security afforded by the rod really outweighs the danger provoked by its supposed active influence in attracting and bringing down a large flash of lightning. In all cases, where the matter has been properly investigated, it has been found that the conductors have been ignorantly and wrongly applied. Either the continuity of the conductor between its termination and the earth has been broken by the presence of rust at the joints, or by the iron connections under ground rusting away ; by the rod itself being broken ; or by the too common careless or ignorant mode of not bringing the end of the conductor properly to earth. It is the opinion of many that if the rod is merely buried a foot or two in the ground it is all that is required. We shall presently see this is by no means sufficient.

4. There is an opinion widely spread, and due in a great measure to the use of the terms "thunderbolt" and "electric fluid," by many writers on electricity, that a small rod of copper, from $\frac{1}{4}$ inch to 1 inch diameter, is totally inadequate to carry off such a large quantity of "fluid" sufficiently rapidly and safely as is supposed to exist when a large flash of lightning is observed.

5. Many persons point to buildings, such as the dome of St. Paul's cathedral, as not being provided with any external special conductor, yet which have escaped being struck in very severe storms. In most of these cases, by the arrangement of the materials of which it is constructed, the building itself is a first-rate conductor, in some cases for a certain height only and in

others from the summit to the ground. St. Paul's is now fitted with copper rope conductors.

In applying a lightning conductor to a chimney or other similar structure, the principles to be kept in view are—

1. To use the best available material; that is, which acts best as a conductor of electricity, and resists corrosion. This material is copper.

2. To provide an adequate sectional area to lead the electricity harmlessly away. This is best arrived at by experience. Harris, in 1861, after citing a number of cases of terrific tropical thunderstorms, concludes that a copper rod $\frac{3}{4}$ in. diameter, or an equal quantity of copper under any other form, would resist the heating effect of any discharge of lightning which has yet come within the experience of mankind. Faraday considered a $\frac{1}{2}$ in. copper rod sufficient, but of course approved of using $\frac{5}{8}$ or $\frac{3}{4}$ in. rods when the expense was not too great.

3. It should be made in such a manner as to run the least risk of having its continuity interrupted in the event of its being fractured. With this object in view, rope is better than rods, since it can be made in the first place in one continuous length, whereby the risk of badly formed joints is avoided; it can be readily coiled and carried to its destination without being cut; and, in the event of being roughly used, the breakage of one or more strands does not destroy the efficiency of the remainder. When joints are used they should be formed by screwing the ends right and left-handed, and bringing them in close contact by a screwed copper socket of ample strength.

The conductor should be supported or suspended in

such a manner as not to risk its fracture by settlement of
the structure or disturbance of one or more of its sup-
ports or guides.

4. The upper extremity should project above the top
of the chimney to a distance, say, equal to the diameter
of the chimney top, and should terminate in a brush of
three or four points arranged round the central terminal, and curved to project therefrom at an angle of
about 45°.

5. As a rule the rod should be placed inside the
structure in the case of a monument, where it is less
liable to be damaged, and is in a better general position for protecting the building, besides being out of
sight. But for a chimney the rod should always be
outside, as the gases from some coals are liable to cor-
rode copper and iron rapidly wherever they come in
contact with these metals, especially in the presence
of moisture.

6 To prevent lateral discharge the conductor should
be in communication with all hoops or pieces of metal
round the chimney, and the use of all insulated pieces
of metal, especially arranged parallel to the conductor,
should be avoided.

7. The rod should terminate in the ground in two or
more branches, which should be carried into a well, and
terminate in a large copper plate, or be connected with
a water drain (made of metal, and not fireclay), or pump,
water or gas pipes, or any other good conducting chan-
nel. Where this is not practicable, the several branches
should be carried into earth that is permanently moist,
and end in a cast-iron case filled with coke, or cinders ;
or have a large copper plate terminal ; or where no
moist earth exists permanently the branches under-

ground should have plenty of length, say 30 feet or more, according to the nature of the ground and size of rod. If no earth-plate is used, the wires of the copper rope should be unstranded and spread out.

When placed outside the chimney the rod may be brought down in contact with the stone or brick-work, and no insulating means are required. A flash of lightning has sufficient intensity to break through miles of air in some cases, hence an attempt at insulation a few inches or even feet in length can have no practical effect in preventing it from striking the brick-work in case the rod should prove insufficient to carry it safely away.

The earth terminal of the rod—unlike the rod itself—should expose as much surface to the soil as possible, because this surface is the measure of the section of solid earth employed to carry off the discharge. Many authorities have advocated the use of a ball instead of a point at the top of the rod, the former being considered best for attracting the lightning from the building; a point is, however, far better for drawing off the electricity, as it does so quietly, and without sparks, and would commence its neutralising effect long before a ball would act, and by so doing might be the means of preventing a violent discharge altogether. In considering the advantages claimed for the ball top, it must not be forgotten that in comparison with the vast area of most electrified thunder clouds, the largest ball, the use of which could be contemplated, must be, after all, a mere point. Although many cases of fusion of copper points are recorded, this material should be still used in preference to iron for the points of conductors, although iron has a higher point of fusion.

All combinations of copper and iron in contact should be avoided, especially when the smaller part of the combination is of iron, to avoid the rapid destruction of the iron by galvanic action, which is but too likely to occur; for instance, iron nails, spikes, staples, &c., should not be brought in contact with the copper rod to support it.

Notwithstanding that water or gas pipes of iron, placed a few feet from a conductor where it reaches the ground, have been broken by the lightning springing to them from the conductor, it yet appears to be the safest plan to connect the conductor with such pipes. In some cases the breakage has been doubtless due to explosion of the steam formed by the intense heat of the lightning current on meeting with the comparatively greater resistance of the ground between the conductor and the pipes. Where there is no resistance offered to the passage of the current no heat or violent effect will ensue.

In a previous paragraph we have spoken of the importance of terminating the rod in "good earth." Upon this depends the value of the lightning rod. Most of the accidents which have taken place—where conductors have been on the building—can be accounted for by insufficient earth connection. A lightning rod when fixed should be tested by a galvanometer, and the "earth" should be tested at least once a year.

A very portable galvanometer for testing lightning conductors has recently been introduced by Mr. Richard Anderson, M.S.T.E., F.C.S., of 101, Leadenhall Street, London.

The following woodcut shows the arrangement of the battery, galvanometer, and resistance coils. The battery consists of three cells, and is a modification of the old manganese cell, in which the carbon and oxide of manganese occupy the outer

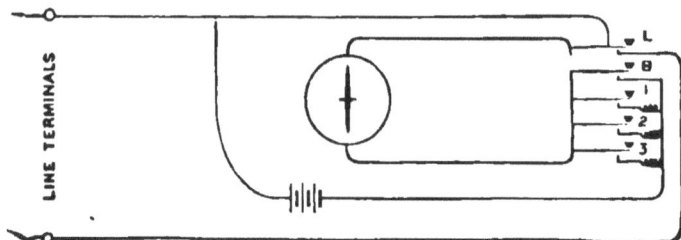

and the zinc plate the inner or porous cell. By this arrangement (introduced a few years ago by Mr. H. Yeats, of Covent Garden), the surface of the negative element is greatly increased, and hence a more constant

current is obtained, on account of the battery not
polarising so rapidly as in the old form. Another advantage of this arrangement is that the cells can be
almost entirely sealed up, the air openings being made
within the porous cell. In the centre of the lid of the
box is placed the galvanometer with a "tangent"
scale. On the left are two terminals by which to connect the conductor to be examined. On the right-
hand end of the lid are placed five keys, marked re-
pectively, L, B, 1, 2, 3. Under B is one pole of the
battery, so that by depressing this key, as will be seen
by following the connections in the diagram, the battery current is sent through the galvanometer direct.
If, however, we depress key No. 1, we connect the
battery with the galvanometer through a known resistance. Key No. 2 has a larger resistance, and No. 3
still larger. The fifth key, L, closes the circuit within
the limit of the instrument, but on being depressed
opens it and includes the line or conductor placed between the two terminals at the other end. On pressing
down L and B, it will be seen that the resistance of the
line or conductor may be compared with the known resistance connected with any of the keys Nos. 1, 2, 3, or
any of these resistances may be included with that of
the line, so as to get a convenient deflection of the galvanometer needle.

In the case with the battery is a bobbin of insulated
wire for connecting the instrument with the conductor
and earth to be tested.

BRADBURY, AGNEW, & CO. LD., PRINTERS, LONDON AND TONBRIDGE.

CROSBY LOCKWOOD & SON'S
Catalogue of
Scientific, Technical and Industrial Books.

MECHANICAL ENGINEERING, ETC.

THE MECHANICAL ENGINEER'S POCKET-BOOK.

Comprising Tables, Formulæ, Rules, and Data : A Handy Book of Reference for Daily Use in Engineering Practice. By D. KINNEAR CLARK, M.Inst. C.E., Fifth Edition, thoroughly Revised and Enlarged. By H. H. P. POWLES, A.M.I.C.E., M.I.M.E. Small 8vo, 700 pp., bound in flexible Leather Cover, rounded corners. *[Just Published.* Net **6/0**

SUMMARY OF CONTENTS :—MATHEMATICAL TABLES.—MEASUREMENT OF SURFACES AND SOLIDS.—ENGLISH WEIGHTS AND MEASURES.—FRENCH METRIC WEIGHTS AND MEASURES.—FOREIGN WEIGHTS AND MEASURES.—MONEYS.—SPECIFIC GRAVITY, WEIGHT, AND VOLUME.—MANUFACTURED METALS.—STEEL PIPES.—BOLTS AND NUTS.— SUNDRY ARTICLES IN WROUGHT AND CAST IRON, COPPER, BRASS, LEAD, TIN, ZINC.— STRENGTH OF MATERIALS. — STRENGTH OF TIMBER.—STRENGTH OF CAST IRON.— STRENGTH OF WROUGHT IRON.—STRENGTH OF STEEL.—TENSILE STRENGTH OF COPPER, LEAD, &c.—RESISTANCE OF STONES AND OTHER BUILDING MATERIALS.—RIVETED JOINTS IN BOILER PLATES.—BOILER SHELLS.—WIRE ROPES AND HEMP ROPES.—CHAINS AND CHAIN CABLES.—FRAMING.—HARDNESS OF METALS, ALLOYS, AND STONES.—LABOUR OF ANIMALS.—MECHANICAL PRINCIPLES.—GRAVITY AND FALL OF BODIES.—ACCELERATING AND RETARDING FORCES.—MILL GEARING, SHAFTING, &c.—TRANSMISSION OF MOTIVE POWER.—HEAT.—COMBUSTION: FUELS.—WARMING, VENTILATION, COOKING STOVES.— STEAM.—STEAM ENGINES AND BOILERS.—RAILWAYS.—TRAMWAYS.—STEAM SHIPS.— PUMPING STEAM ENGINES AND PUMPS.—COAL GAS, GAS ENGINES, &c.—AIR IN MOTION. —COMPRESSED AIR.—HOT AIR ENGINES.—WATER POWER.—SPEED OF CUTTING TOOLS. —COLOURS.—ELECTRICAL ENGINEERING.

"Mr. Clark manifests what is an innate perception of what is likely to be useful in a pocket-book, and he is really unrivalled in the art of condensation. It is very difficult to hit upon any mechanical engineering subject concerning which this work supplies no information, and the excellent index at the end adds to its utility. In one word, it is an exceedingly handy and efficient tool, possessed of which the engineer will be saved many a wearisome calculation, or yet more wearisome hunt through various text-books and treatises, and, as such, we can heartily recommend it to our readers."—*The Engineer.*

"It would be found difficult to compress more matter within a similar compass, or produce a book of 700 pages which should be more compact or convenient for pocket reference. . . . Will be appreciated by mechanical engineers of all classes."—*Practical Engineer.*

L.   A

MR. HUTTON'S PRACTICAL HANDBOOKS.

THE WORKS' MANAGER'S HANDBOOK.

Comprising Modern Rules, Tables, and Data. For Engineers, Millwrights, and Boiler Makers; Tool Makers, Machinists, and Metal Workers; Iron and Brass Founders, &c. By W. S. HUTTON, Civil and Mechanical Engineer, Author of "The Practical Engineer's Handbook." Sixth Edition, carefully Revised, and Enlarged. In One handsome Volume, medium 8vo, strongly bound **15/0**

☛ *The Author having compiled Rules and Data for his own use in a great variety of modern engineering work, and having found his notes extremely useful, decided to publish them—revised to date—believing that a practical work, suited to the* DAILY REQUIREMENTS OF MODERN ENGINEERS, *would be favourably received.*

"Of this edition we may repeat the appreciative remarks we made upon the first and third. Since the appearance of the latter very considerable modifications have been made, although the total number of pages remains almost the same. It is a very useful collection of rules, tables, and workshop and drawing office data."—*The Engineer*, May 10, 1895.

"The author treats every subject from the point of view of one who has collected workshop notes for application in workshop practice, rather than from the theoretical or literary aspect. The volume contains a great deal of that kind of information which is gained only by practical experience, and is seldom written in books."—*The Engineer*, June 5, 1885.

"The volume is an exceedingly useful one, brimful with engineer's notes, memoranda, and rules, and well worthy of being on every mechanical engineer's bookshelf."—*Mechanical World*.

"The information is precisely that likely to be required in practice. . . . The work forms a desirable addition to the library not only of the works' manager, but of any one connected with general engineering."—*Mining Journal*.

"Brimful of useful information, stated in a concise form. Mr. Hutton's books have met a pressing want among engineers. The book must prove extremely useful to every practical man possessing a copy."—*Practical Engineer*.

THE PRACTICAL ENGINEER'S HANDBOOK.

Comprising a Treatise on Modern Engines and Boilers, Marine, Locomotive, and Stationary. And containing a large collection of Rules and Practical Data relating to Recent Practice in Designing and Constructing all kinds of Engines, Boilers, and other Engineering work. The whole constituting a comprehensive Key to the Board of Trade and other Examinations for Certificates of Competency in Modern Mechanical Engineering. By WALTER S. HUTTON, Civil and Mechanical Engineer, Author of "The Works' Manager's Handbook for Engineers," &c. With upwards of 420 Illustrations. Sixth Edition. Revised and Enlarged. Medium 8vo, nearly 560 pp., strongly bound. **18/0**

☛ *This Work is designed as a companion to the Author's "WORKS' MANAGER'S HANDBOOK." It possesses many new and original features, and contains, like its predecessor, a quantity of matter not originally intended for publication but collected by the Author for his own use in the construction of a great variety of* MODERN ENGINEERING WORK.

The information is given in a condensed and concise form, and is illustrated by upwards of 420 Engravings; and comprises a quantity of tabulated matter of great value to all engaged in designing, constructing, or estimating for ENGINES, BOILERS, *and* OTHER ENGINEERING WORK.

"We have kept it at hand for several weeks, referring to it as occasion arose, and we have not on a single occasion consulted its pages without finding the information of which we were in quest."—*Athenaeum*.

"A thoroughly good practical handbook, which no engineer can go through without learning something that will be of service to him."—*Marine Engineer*.

"An excellent book of reference for engineers, and a valuable text-book for students of engineering."—*Scotsman*.

"This valuable manual embodies the results and experience of the leading authorities on mechanical engineering."—*Building News*.

"The author has collected together a surprising quantity of rules and practical data, and has shown much judgment in the selections he has made. . . . There is no doubt that this book is one of the most useful of its kind published, and will be a very popular compendium."—*Engineer*.

"A mass of information set down in simple language, and in such a form that it can be easily referred to at any time. The matter is uniformly good and well chosen, and is greatly elucidated by the illustrations. The book will find its way on to most engineers' shelves, where it will rank as one of the most useful books of reference."—*Practical Engineer*.

"Full of useful information, and should be found on the office shelf of all practical engineers."—*English Mechanic*.

MR. HUTTON'S PRACTICAL HANDBOOKS—*continued.*

STEAM BOILER CONSTRUCTION.

A Practical Handbook for Engineers, Boiler-Makers, and Steam Users. Containing a large Collection of Rules and Data relating to Recent Practice in the Design, Construction, and Working of all Kinds of Stationary, Locomotive, and Marine Steam-Boilers. By WALTER S. HUTTON, Civil and Mechanical Engineer, Author of "The Works' Manager's Handbook," "The Practical Engineer's Handbook," &c. With upwards of 500 Illustrations. Fourth Edition, carefully Revised, and Enlarged. Medium 8vo, over 680 pages, cloth, strongly bound. [*Just Published.* **18/0**

☞ THIS WORK *is issued in continuation of the Series of Handbooks written by the Author, viz.* :—"THE WORKS' MANAGER'S HANDBOOK" *and* "THE PRACTICAL ENGINEER'S HANDBOOK," *which are so highly appreciated by engineers for the practical nature of their information; and is consequently written in the same style as those works.*

The Author believes that the concentration, in a convenient form for easy reference, of such a large amount of thoroughly practical information on Steam-Boilers, will be of considerable service to those for whom it is intended, and he trusts the book may be deemed worthy of as favourable a reception as has been accorded to its predecessors.

"One of the best, if not the best, books on boilers that has ever been published. The information is of the right kind, in a simple and accessible form. So far as generation is concerned, this is, undoubtedly, the standard book on steam practice."—*Electrical Review.*
"Every detail, both in boiler design and management, is clearly laid before the reader. The volume shows that boiler construction has been reduced to the condition of one of the most exact sciences; and such a book is of the utmost value to the *fin de siècle* Engineer and Works Manager."—*Marine Engineer.*
"There has long been room for a modern handbook on steam boilers; there is not that room now, because Mr. Hutton has filled it. It is a thoroughly practical book for those who are occupied in the construction, design, selection, or use of boilers."—*Engineer.*
"The book is of so important and comprehensive a character that it must find its way into the libraries of every one interested in boiler using or boiler manufacture if they wish to be thoroughly informed. We strongly recommend the book for the intrinsic value of its contents."—*Machinery Market.*

PRACTICAL MECHANICS' WORKSHOP COMPANION.

Comprising a great variety of the most useful Rules and Formulæ in Mechanical Science, with numerous Tables of Practical Data and Calculated Results for Facilitating Mechanical Operations. By WILLIAM TEMPLETON, Author of "The Engineer's Practical Assistant," &c., &c. Eighteenth Edition, Revised, Modernised, and considerably Enlarged by WALTER S. HUTTON, C.E., Author of "The Works' Manager's Handbook," "The Practical Engineer's Handbook," &c. Fcap. 8vo, nearly 500 pp., with 8 Plates and upwards of 250 Illustrative Diagrams, strongly bound for workshop or pocket wear and tear. **6/0**

"In its modernised form Hutton's 'Templeton' should have a wide sale, for it contains much valuable information which the mechanic will often find of use, and not a few tables and notes which he might look for in vain in other works. This modernised edition will be appreciated by all who have learned to value the original editions of 'Templeton.'"—*English Mechanic.*
"It has met with great success in the engineering workshop, as we can testify; and there are a great many men who, in a great measure, owe their rise in life to this little book."—*Building News.*
"This familiar text-book—well known to all mechanics and engineers—is of essential service to the every-day requirements of engineers, millwrights, and the various trades connected with engineering and building. The new modernised edition is worth its weight in gold."—*Building News.* (Second Notice.)
"This well-known and largely-used book contains information, brought up to date, of the sort so useful to the foreman and draughtsman. So much fresh information has been introduced as to constitute it practically a new book. It will be largely used in the office and workshop."—*Mechanical World.*
"The publishers wisely entrusted the task of revision of this popular, valuable, and useful book to Mr. Hutton, than whom a more competent man they could not have found."—*Iron.*

ENGINEER'S AND MILLWRIGHT'S ASSISTANT.

A Collection of Useful Tables, Rules, and Data. By WILLIAM TEMPLETON. Eighth Edition, with Additions. 18mo, cloth **2/6**

"Occupies a foremost place among books of this kind. A more suitable present to an apprentice to any of the mechanical trades could not possibly be made."—*Building News.*
"A deservedly popular work. It should be in the 'drawer' of every mechanic."—*English Mechanic.*

A 2

THE MECHANICAL ENGINEER'S REFERENCE BOOK.

For Machine and Boiler Construction. In Two Parts. Part I. GENERAL ENGINEERING DATA. Part II. BOILER CONSTRUCTION. With 51 Plates and numerous Illustrations. By NELSON FOLEY, M.I.N.A. Second Edition, Revised throughout and much Enlarged. Folio, half-bound. *Net* **£3 3s.**

PART I.—MEASURES.—CIRCUMFERENCES AND AREAS, &c., SQUARES, CUBES, FOURTH POWERS.—SQUARE AND CUBE ROOTS.—SURFACE OF TUBES.—RECIPROCALS.— LOGARITHMS. — MENSURATION. — SPECIFIC GRAVITIES AND WEIGHTS.—WORK AND POWER. — HEAT. — COMBUSTION.—EXPANSION AND CONTRACTION. —EXPANSION OF GASES.—STEAM.— STATIC FORCES.—GRAVITATION AND ATTRACTION.—MOTION AND COMPUTATION OF RESULTING FORCES.—ACCUMULATED WORK.—CENTRE AND RADIUS OF GYRATION.—MOMENT OF INERTIA.—CENTRE OF OSCILLATION.—ELECTRICITY.— STRENGTH OF MATERIALS.—ELASTICITY.—TEST SHEETS OF METALS.—FRICTION.— TRANSMISSION OF POWER.—FLOW OF LIQUIDS.—FLOW OF GASES.— AIR PUMPS, SURFACE CONDENSERS, &c.—SPEED OF STEAMSHIPS.—PROPELLERS.—CUTTING TOOLS.—FLANGES. —COPPER SHEETS AND TUBES.—SCREWS, NUTS, BOLT HEADS, &c.—VARIOUS RECIPES AND MISCELLANEOUS MATTER.—WITH DIAGRAMS FOR VALVE-GEAR, BELTING AND ROPES, DISCHARGE AND SUCTION PIPES, SCREW PROPELLERS, AND COPPER PIPES.

PART II.—TREATING OF POWER OF BOILERS.—USEFUL RATIOS.—NOTES ON CONSTRUCTION. — CYLINDRICAL BOILER SHELLS. — CIRCULAR FURNACES. — FLAT PLATES.—STAYS. — GIRDERS.—SCREWS. — HYDRAULIC TESTS. — RIVETING. — BOILER SETTING, CHIMNEYS, AND MOUNTINGS.—FUELS, &c.—EXAMPLES OF BOILERS AND SPEEDS OF STEAMSHIPS.—NOMINAL AND NORMAL HORSE POWER.—WITH DIAGRAMS FOR ALL BOILER CALCULATIONS AND DRAWINGS OF MANY VARIETIES OF BOILERS.

"Mr. Foley is well fitted to compile such a work. The diagrams are a great feature of the work. It may be stated that Mr. Foley has produced a volume which will undoubtedly fulfil the desire of the author and become indispensable to all mechanical engineers."—*Marine Engineer.*

"We have carefully examined this work, and pronounce it a most excellent reference book for the use of marine engineers."—*Journal of American Society of Naval Engineers.*

TEXT-BOOK ON THE STEAM ENGINE.

With a Supplement on GAS ENGINES and PART II. on HEAT ENGINES. By T. M. GOODEVE, M.A., Barrister-at-Law, Professor of Mechanics at the Royal College of Science, London ; Author of "The Principles of Mechanics," "The Elements of Mechanism," &c. Fourteenth Edition. Crown 8vo, cloth . **6/0**

"Professor Goodeve has given us a treatise on the steam engine which will bear comparison with anything written by Huxley or Maxwell, and we can award it no higher praise."—*Engineer.*
"Mr. Goodeve's text-book is a work of which every young engineer should possess himself." —*Mining Journal.*

ON GAS ENGINES.

With Appendix describing a Recent Engine with Tube Igniter. By T. M. GOODEVE, M.A. Crown 8vo, cloth **2/6**

"Like all Mr. Goodeve's writings, the present is no exception in point of general excellence. It is a valuable little volume."—*Mechanical World.*

GAS AND OIL ENGINE MANAGEMENT.

A Practical Guide for Users and Attendants, being Notes on Selection, Construction, and Management. By M. POWIS BALE, M.I M.E., A.M.I.C.E. Author of "Woodworking Machinery," &c. Crown 8vo, cloth.
[*Just Published. Net* **3 6**

THE GAS-ENGINE HANDBOOK.

A Manual of Useful Information for the Designer and the Engineer. By E. W. ROBERTS, M.E. With Forty Full-page Engravings. Small Fcap. 8vo, leather.
Net **8/6**

A TREATISE ON STEAM BOILERS.

Their Strength, Construction, and Economical Working. By R. WILSON, C.E. Fifth Edition. 12mo, cloth **6/0**

"The best treatise that has ever been published on steam boilers."—*Engineer.*

THE MECHANICAL ENGINEER'S COMPANION

of Areas, Circumferences, Decimal Equivalents, in inches and feet, millimetres, squares, cubes, roots, &c. ; Strength of Bolts, Weight of Iron, &c. ; Weights, Measures, and other Data. Also Practical Rules for Engine Proportions. By R. EDWARDS, M.Inst.C.E. Fcap. 8vo, cloth. **3/6**

"A very useful little volume. It contains many tables, classified data and memoranda generally useful to engineers."—*Engineer.*

"What it professes to be, ' a handy office companion,' giving in a succinct form, a variety of information likely to be required by mechanical engineers in their everyday office work."—*Nature.*

A HANDBOOK ON THE STEAM ENGINE.

With especial Reference to Small and Medium-sized Engines. For the Use of Engine Makers, Mechanical Draughtsmen, Engineering Students, and users of Steam Power. By HERMAN HAEDER, C.E. Translated from the German with additions and alterations, by H. H. P. POWLES, A.M.I.C.E.. M.I.M.E. Third Edition, Revised. With nearly 1,100 Illustrations. Crown 8vo, cloth   .   .   .   .   *Net* **7/6**

"A perfect encyclopædia of the steam engine and its details, and one which must take a permanent place in English drawing-offices and workshops."—*A Foreman Pattern-maker.*
"This is an excellent book, and should be in the hands of all who are interested in the construction and design of medium-sized stationary engines. . . . A careful study of its contents and the arrangement of the sections leads to the conclusion that there is probably no other book like it in this country. The volume aims at showing the results of practical experience, and it certainly may claim a complete achievement of this idea."—*Nature.*
"There can be no question as to its value. We cordially commend it to all concerned in the design and construction of the steam engine."—*Mechanical World.*

BOILER AND FACTORY CHIMNEYS.

Their Draught-Power and Stability. With a chapter on *Lightning Conductors.* By ROBERT WILSON, A.I.C.E., Author of "A Treatise on Steam Boilers," &c. Crown 8vo, cloth **3/6**

"A valuable contribution to the literature of scientific building."—*The Builder.*

BOILER MAKER'S READY RECKONER & ASSISTANT.

With Examples of Practical Geometry and Templating, for the Use of Platers, Smiths, and Riveters. By JOHN COURTNEY, Edited by D. K. CLARK, M.I.C.E. Fourth Edition, 480 pp., with 140 Illustrations. Fcap. 8vo, half-bound **7/0**

"No workman or apprentice should be without this book."—*Iron Trade Circular.*

REFRIGERATION, COLD STORAGE, & ICE-MAKING:

A Practical Treatise on the Art and Science of Refrigeration. By A. J. WALLIS-TAYLER, A.M.Inst.C.E., Author of "Refrigerating and Ice-Making Machinery." 600 pp., with 360 Illustrations. Medium 8vo, cloth. *Net* **15/0**

"The author has to be congratulated on the completion and production of such an important work and it cannot fail to have a large body of readers, for it leaves out nothing that would in any way be of value to those interested in the subject."—*Steamship.*
"No one whose duty it is to handle the mammoth preserving installations of these latter days can afford to be without this valuable book."—*Glasgow Herald.*

THE POCKET BOOK OF REFRIGERATION AND ICE-MAKING.

Edited by A. J. WALLIS-TAYLER, A.M.Inst.C.E. Author of "Refrigerating and Ice-making Machinery," &c. Small Crown 8vo, cloth.

[*Just Published. Net* **3/6**

REFRIGERATING & ICE-MAKING MACHINERY.

A Descriptive Treatise for the Use of Persons Employing Refrigerating and Ice-Making Installations, and others. By A. J. WALLIS-TAYLER, A.-M. Inst. C.E. Third Edition, Enlarged. Crown 8vo, cloth .   .   **7/6**

"Practical, explicit, and profusely illustrated."—*Glasgow Herald.*
"We recommend the book, which gives the cost of various systems and illustrations showing details of parts of machinery and general arrangements of complete installations."—*Builder.*
"May be recommended as a useful description of the machinery, the processes, and of the facts, figures, and tabulated physics of refrigerating. It is one of the best compilations on the subject."—*Engineer.*

ENGINEERING ESTIMATES, COSTS, AND ACCOUNTS.

A Guide to Commercial Engineering. With numerous examples of Estimates and Costs of Millwright Work, Miscellaneous Productions, Steam Engines and Steam Boilers; and a Section on the Preparation of Costs Accounts. By A GENERAL MANAGER. Second Edition. 8vo, cloth. **12/0**

"This is an excellent and very useful book, covering subject-matter in constant requisition in every factory and workshop. . . . The book is invaluable, not only to the young engineer, but also to the estimate department of every works."—*Builder.*
"We accord the work unqualified praise. The information is given in a plain, straightforward manner, and bears throughout evidence of the intimate practical acquaintance of the author with every phase of commercial engineering."—*Mechanical World.*

HOISTING MACHINERY.

An Elementary Treatise on. Including the Elements of Crane Construction and Descriptions of the Various Types of Cranes in Use. By JOSEPH HORNER, A.M.I.M.E., Author of "Pattern-Making," and other Works. Crown 8vo, with 215 Illustrations, including Folding Plates, cloth.

[Just Published. Net **7/6**

AERIAL OR WIRE-ROPE TRAMWAYS.

Their Construction and Management. By A. J. WALLIS-TAYLER, A.M. Inst. C.E. With 81 Illustrations. Crown 8vo, cloth **7/6**

"This is in its way an excellent volume. Without going into the minutiæ of the subject, it yet lays before its readers a very good exposition of the various systems of rope transmission in use, and gives as well not a little valuable information about their working, repair, and management. We can safely recommend it as a useful general treatise on the subject."—*The Engineer.*

MOTOR CARS OR POWER-CARRIAGES FOR COMMON ROADS.

By A. J. WALLIS-TAYLER, A. M. Inst. C.E., Author of "Modern Cycles," &c. 212 pp., with 76 Illustrations. Crown 8vo, cloth **4/6**

"The book is clearly expressed throughout, and is just the sort of work that an engineer thinking of turning his attention to motor-carriage work, would do well to read as a preliminary to starting operations."—*Engineering.*

PLATING AND BOILER MAKING.

A Practical Handbook for Workshop Operations. By JOSEPH G. HORNER, A.M.I.M.E. 380 pp. with 338 Illustrations. Crown 8vo, cloth . . **7/6**

"This work is characterised by that evidence of close acquaintance with workshop methods which will render the book exceedingly acceptable to the practical hand. We have no hesitation in commending the work as a serviceable and practical handbook on a subject which has not hitherto received much attention from those qualified to deal with it in a satisfactory manner."—*Mechanical World.*

PATTERN MAKING.

A Practical Treatise, embracing the Main Types of Engineering Construction, and including Gearing, Engine Work, Sheaves and Pulleys, Pipes and Columns, Screws, Machine Parts, Pumps and Cocks, the Moulding of Patterns in Loam and Greensand, estimating the weight of Castings &c. By JOSEPH G. HORNER, A.M.I.M.E. Third Edition, Enlarged. With 486 Illustrations. Crown 8vo, cloth. *Net* **7/6**

"A well-written technical guide, evidently written by a man who understands and has practised what he has written about. . . . We cordially recommend it to engineering students, young journeymen, and others desirous of being initiated into the mysteries of pattern-making."—*Builder.*
"An excellent *vade mecum* for the apprentice who desires to become master of his trade."
—*English Mechanic.*

MECHANICAL ENGINEERING TERMS

(Lockwood's Dictionary of). Embracing those current in the Drawing Office, Pattern Shop, Foundry, Fitting, Turning, Smiths', and Boiler Shops, &c. Comprising upwards of 6,000 Definitions. Edited by J. G. HORNER, A.M.I.M.E. Third Edition, Revised, with Additions. Crown 8vo, cloth . . *Net* **7/6**

"Just the sort of handy dictionary required by the various trades engaged in mechanical engineering. The practical engineering pupil will find the book of great value in his studies, and every foreman engineer and mechanic should have a copy."—*Building News.*

TOOTHED GEARING.

A Practical Handbook for Offices and Workshops. By J. HORNER, A.M.I.M.E. With 184 Illustrations. Crown 8vo, cloth **6/0**

"We give the book our unqualified praise for its thoroughness of treatment, and recommend it to all interested as the most practical book on the subject yet written."—*Mechanical World.*

FIRES, FIRE-ENGINES, AND FIRE BRIGADES.

With a History of Fire-Engines, their Construction, Use, and Management; Foreign Fire Systems; Hints on Fire-Brigades, &c. By C. F. T. YOUNG, C.E. 8vo, cloth . . . . **£1 4s.**

"To such of our readers as are interested in the subject of fires and fire apparatus we can most heartily commend this book."—*Engineering.*

AËRIAL NAVIGATION.

A Practical Handbook on the Construction of Dirigible Balloons, Aërostats, Aëroplanes, and Aëremotors. By FREDERICK WALKER, C.E., Associate Member of the Aëronautic Institute. With 104 Illustrations. Large Crown 8vo, cloth . . . . *Net* **7/6**

STONE-WORKING MACHINERY.

A Manual dealing with the Rapid and Economical Conversion of Stone. With Hints on the Arrangement and Management of Stone Works. By M. POWIS BALE, M.I.M.E. Second Edition, enlarged. Crown 8vo, cloth . . **9/0**

"The book should be in the hands of every mason or student of stonework."—*Colliery Guardian.*
"A capital handbook for all who manipulate stone for building or ornamental purposes."—*Machinery Market.*

PUMPS AND PUMPING.

A Handbook for Pump Users. Being Notes on Selection, Construction, and Management. By M. POWIS BALE, M.I.M.E. Fourth Edition. Crown 8vo, cloth **3/6**

"The matter is set forth as concisely as possible. In fact, condensation rather than diffuseness has been the author's aim throughout; yet he does not seem to have omitted anything likely to be of use."—*Journal of Gas Lighting.*
"Thoroughly practical and clearly written."—*Glasgow Herald.*

MILLING MACHINES AND PROCESSES.

A Practical Treatise on Shaping Metals by Rotary Cutters. Including Information on Making and Grinding the Cutters. By PAUL N. HASLUCK, Author of "Lathe-Work." With upwards of 300 Engravings. Large crown 8vo, cloth **12/6**

"A new departure in engineering literature. . . . We can recommend this work to all interested in milling machines; it is what it professes to be—a practical treatise."—*Engineer.*
"A capital and reliable book which will no doubt be of considerable service both to those who are already acquainted with the process as well as to those who contemplate its adoption."—*Industries.*

LATHE-WORK.

A Practical Treatise on the Tools, Appliances, and Processes employed in the Art of Turning. By PAUL N. HASLUCK. Eighth Edition. Crown 8vo, cloth **5/0**

"Written by a man who knows not only how work ought to be done, but who also knows how to do it, and how to convey his knowledge to others. To all turners this book would be valuable."—*Engineering.*
"We can safely recommend the work to young engineers. To the amateur it will simply be invaluable. To the student it will convey a great deal of useful information."—*Engineer.*

SCREW-THREADS,

And Methods of Producing Them. With numerous Tables and complete Directions for using Screw-Cutting Lathes. By PAUL N. HASLUCK, Author of "Lathe-Work," &c. Sixth Edition. Waistcoat-pocket size . . **1/6**

"Full of useful information, hints and practical criticism. Taps, dies, and screwing tools generally are illustrated and their action described."—*Mechanical World.*
"It is a complete compendium of all the details of the screw-cutting lathe; in fact, a *multum-in-parvo* on all the subjects it treats upon."—*Carpenter and Builder.*

TABLES AND MEMORANDA FOR ENGINEERS, MECHANICS, ARCHITECTS, BUILDERS, &c.

Selected and Arranged by FRANCIS SMITH. Seventh Edition, Revised, including ELECTRICAL TABLES, FORMULÆ, and MEMORANDA. Waistcoat-pocket size, limp leather. [*Just Published.* **1/6**

"It would, perhaps, be as difficult to make a small pocket-book selection of notes and formulæ to suit ALL engineers as it would be to make a universal medicine; but Mr. Smith's waistcoat-pocket collection may be looked upon as a successful attempt."—*Engineer.*
"The best example we have ever seen of 270 pages of useful matter packed into the dimensions of a card-case."—*Building News.* "A veritable pocket treasury of knowledge."—*Iron.*

POCKET GLOSSARY OF TECHNICAL TERMS.

English-French, French-English; with Tables suitable for the Architectural, Engineering, Manufacturing, and Nautical Professions. By JOHN JAMES FLETCHER. Third Edition, 200 pp. Waistcoat-pocket size, limp leather **1/6**

"It is a very great advantage for readers and correspondents in France and England to have so large a number of the words relating to engineering and manufacturers collected in a lilliputian volume. The little book will be useful both to students and travellers."—*Architect.*
"The glossary of terms is very complete, and many of the Tables are new and well arranged. We cordially commend the book."—*Mechanical World.*

THE ENGINEER'S YEAR BOOK FOR 1904.

Comprising Formulæ, Rules, Tables, Data and Memoranda in Civil, Mechanical, Electrical, Marine and Mine Engineering. By H. R. KEMPE, A.M. Inst. C.E., M.I.E.E., Principal Technical Officer, Engineer-in-Chief's Office, General Post Office, London, Author of "A Handbook of Electrical Testing," "The Electrical Engineer's Pocket-Book," &c. With 1,000 Illustrations, specially Engraved for the work. Crown 8vo, 900 pp., leather. [*Just Published.* **8/0**

"Kempe's Year Book really requires no commendation. Its sphere of usefulness is widely known, and it is used by engineers the world over."—*The Engineer.*

"The volume is distinctly in advance of most similar publications in this country."—*Engineering.*

"This valuable and well-designed book of reference meets the demands of all descriptions of engineers."—*Saturday Review.*

"Teems with up-to-date information in every branch of engineering and construction."—*Building News.*

"The needs of the engineering profession could hardly be supplied in a more admirable, complete and convenient form. To say that it more than sustains all comparisons is praise of the highest sort, and that may justly be said of it."—*Mining Journal.*

"There is certainly room for the newcomer, which supplies explanations and directions, as well as formulæ and tables. It deserves to become one of the most successful of the technical annuals."—*Architect.*

"Brings together with great skill all the technical information which an engineer has to use day by day. It is in every way admirably equipped, and is sure to prove successful."—*Scotsman.*

"The up-to-dateness of Mr. Kempe's compilation is a quality that will not be lost on the busy people for whom the work is intended."—*Glasgow Herald.*

THE PORTABLE ENGINE.

A Practical Manual on its Construction and Management. For the use of Owners and Users of Steam Engines generally. By WILLIAM DYSON WANSBROUGH. Crown 8vo, cloth **3/6**

"This is a work of value to those who use steam machinery. . . . Should be read by every one who has a steam engine, on a farm or elsewhere."—*Mark Lane Express.*

IRON AND STEEL.

A Work for the Forge, Foundry, Factory, and Office. Containing ready, useful, and trustworthy Information for Ironmasters and their Stock-takers; Managers of Bar, Rail, Plate, and Sheet Rolling Mills; Iron and Metal Founders; Iron Ship and Bridge Builders; Mechanical, Mining, and Consulting Engineers; Architects, Contractors, Builders, &c. By CHARLES HOARE, Author of "The Slide Rule," &c. Ninth Edition. 32mo, leather . **6/0**

CONDENSED MECHANICS.

A Selection of Formulæ, Rules, Tables, and Data or the Use of Engineering Students, &c. By W. G. C. HUGHES, A.M.I.C.E. Crown 8vo, cloth . **2/6**

"The book is well fitted for those who are preparing for examination and wish to refresh their knowledge by going through their formulæ again."—*Marine Engineer.*

THE SAFE USE OF STEAM.

Containing Rules for Unprofessional Steam Users. By an ENGINEER. Seventh Edition. Sewed . . . . **6D.**

"If steam-users would but learn this little book by heart, boiler explosions would become sensations by their rarity."—*English Mechanic.*

THE CARE AND MANAGEMENT OF STATIONARY ENGINES.

A Practical Handbook for Men-in-charge. By C. HURST. Crown 8vo. *Net* **1/0**

THE LOCOMOTIVE ENGINE.

The Autobiography of an Old Locomotive Engine. By ROBERT WEATHERBURN, M.I.M.E. With Illustrations and Portraits of GEORGE and ROBERT STEPHENSON. Crown 8vo, cloth. *Net* **2/6**

THE LOCOMOTIVE ENGINE AND ITS DEVELOPMENT.

A Popular Treatise on the Gradual Improvements made in Railway Engines between 1803 and 1903. By CLEMENT E. STRETTON, C.E. Sixth Edition, Revised and Enlarged. Crown 8vo, cloth. [*Just Published. Net* **4/6**

"Students of railway history and all who are interested in the evolution of the modern locomotive will find much to attract and entertain in this volume."—*The Times.*

MODERN MACHINE SHOP TOOLS,
THEIR CONSTRUCTION, OPERATION, AND MANIPULATION.
Including both Hand and Machine Tools. An entirely New and Fully
Illustrated Work, treating this Subject in a Concise and Comprehensive
Manner. A Book of Practical Instruction in all Classes of Machine Shop
Practice. Including Chapters on Filing, Fitting, and Scraping Surfaces; on
Drills, Reamers, Taps, and Dies; the Lathe and its Tools; Planers, Shapers,
and their Tools; Milling Machines and Cutters; Gear Cutters and Gear
Cutting; Drilling Machines and Drill Work; Grinding Machines and their
Work; Hardening and Tempering, Gearing, Belting, and Transmission
Machinery; Useful Data and Tables. By WILLIAM H. VAN DERVOORT, M.E.
Illustrated by 673 Engravings of Latest Tools and Methods, all of which are
fully described. Medium 8vo, cloth. *[Just Published. Net* **21/0**

LOCOMOTIVE ENGINE DRIVING.
A Practical Manual for Engineers in Charge of Locomotive Engines. By
MICHAEL REYNOLDS, formerly Locomotive Inspector, L. B. & S. C. R.
Eleventh Edition. Including a KEY TO THE LOCOMOTIVE ENGINE.
Crown 8vo, cloth **4/6**
"Mr. Reynolds has supplied a want, and has supplied it well. We can confidently recom-
mend the book not only to the practical driver, but to everyone who takes an interest in the
performance of locomotive engines."—*The Engineer.*
"Mr. Reynolds has opened a new chapter in the literature of the day. This admirable
practical treatise, of the practical utility of which we have to speak in terms of warm commendation."
—*Athenæum.*

THE MODEL LOCOMOTIVE ENGINEER,
Fireman, and Engine-Boy. Comprising a Historical Notice of the Pioneer
Locomotive Engines and their Inventors. By MICHAEL REYNOLDS. Second
Edition, with Revised Appendix. Crown 8vo, cloth. **4/6**
"We should be glad to see this book in the possession of everyone in the kingdom who has
ever laid, or is to lay, hands on a locomotive engine."—*Iron.*

CONTINUOUS RAILWAY BRAKES.
A Practical Treatise on the several Systems in Use in the United Kingdom:
their Construction and Performance. By MICHAEL REYNOLDS. 8vo, cloth
9/0
"A popular explanation of the different brakes. It will be of great assistance in forming
public opinion, and will be studied with benefit by those who take an interest in the brake."—*English
Mechanic.*

STATIONARY ENGINE DRIVING.
A Practical Manual for Engineers in Charge of Stationary Engines. By
MICHAEL REYNOLDS. Sixth Edition. With Plates and Woodcuts.
Crown 8vo, cloth **4/6**
"The author's advice on the various points treated is clear and practical."—*Engineering.*
"Our author leaves no stone unturned. He is determined that his readers shall not only
know something about the stationary engine, but all about it."—*Engineer.*

ENGINE-DRIVING LIFE.
Stirring Adventures and Incidents in the Lives of Locomotive Engine-
Drivers. By MICHAEL REYNOLDS. Third Edition. Crown 8vo, cloth . **1/6**
"From first to last perfectly fascinating. Wilkie Collins's most thrilling conceptions are
thrown into the shade by true incidents, endless in their variety, related in every page."—*North
British Mail.*

THE ENGINEMAN'S POCKET COMPANION,
And Practical Educator for Enginemen, Boiler Attendants, and Mechanics.
By MICHAEL REYNOLDS. With 45 Illustrations and numerous Diagrams
Fourth Edition, Revised. Royal 18mo, strongly bound for pocket wear. **3/6**
"A most meritorious work, giving in a succinct and practical form all the information an
engine-minder desirous of mastering the scientific principles of his daily calling would require."—
The Miller.

CIVIL ENGINEERING, SURVEYING, ETC.

PIONEER IRRIGATION.

A Manual of Information for Farmers in the Colonies. By E. O. MAWSON, Executive Engineer, Public Works Department, Bombay. With Numerous Plates and Diagrams. Medium 8vo, cloth.

[*Just ready. Price about* **7/6** *net.*

SUMMARY OF CONTENTS:—VALUE OF IRRIGATION, AND SOURCES OF WATER SUPPLY.—DAMS AND WEIRS.—CANALS.—UNDERGROUND WATER.—METHODS OF IRRIGATION.—SEWAGE IRRIGATION.—IMPERIAL AUTOMATIC SLUICE GATES.—THE CULTIVATION OF IRRIGATED CROPS, VEGETABLES, AND FRUIT TREES.—LIGHT RAILWAYS FOR HEAVY TRAFFIC.—USEFUL MEMORANDA, TABLES, AND DATA.

TUNNELLING.

A Practical Treatise. By CHARLES PRELINI, C.E. With additions by CHARLES S. HILL, C.E. With 150 Diagrams and Illustrations. Royal 8vo, cloth . . . . *Net* **16/0**

PRACTICAL TUNNELLING.

Explaining in detail Setting-out the Works, Shaft-sinking, and Heading-driving, Ranging the Lines and Levelling underground, Sub-Excavating, Timbering and the Construction of the Brickwork of Tunnels. By F. W. SIMMS, M. Inst. C.E. Fourth Edition, Revised and Further Extended, including the most recent (1895) Examples of Sub-aqueous and other Tunnels, by D. KINNEAR CLARK, M. Inst. C.E. With 34 Folding Plates. Imperial 8vo, cloth **£2 2s.**

"The present (1896) edition has been brought right up to date, and is thus rendered a work to which civil engineers generally should have ready access, and to which engineers who have construction work can hardly afford to be without, but which to the younger members of the profession is invaluable, as from its pages they can learn the state to which the science of tunnelling has attained."—*Railway News.*

THE WATER SUPPLY OF TOWNS AND THE CONSTRUCTION OF WATER-WORKS.

A Practical Treatise for the Use of Engineers and Students of Engineering. By W. K. BURTON, A.M. Inst. C.E., Consulting Engineer to the Tokyo Water-works. Second Edition, Revised and Extended. With numerous Plates and Illustrations. Super-royal 8vo, buckram. [*Just Published.* **25/0**

I. INTRODUCTORY. — II. DIFFERENT QUALITIES OF WATER. — III. QUANTITY OF WATER TO BE PROVIDED.—IV. ON ASCERTAINING WHETHER A PROPOSED SOURCE OF SUPPLY IS SUFFICIENT.—V. ON ESTIMATING THE STORAGE CAPACITY REQUIRED TO BE PROVIDED.—VI. CLASSIFICATION OF WATER-WORKS.—VII. IMPOUNDING RESERVOIRS.—VIII. EARTHWORK DAMS.—IX. MASONRY DAMS.—X. THE PURIFICATION OF WATER.—XI. SETTLING RESERVOIRS.—XII. SAND FILTRATION.—XIII. PURIFICATION OF WATER BY ACTION OF IRON, SOFTENING OF WATER BY ACTION OF LIME, NATURAL FILTRATION.—XIV. SERVICE OR CLEAN WATER RESERVOIRS—WATER TOWERS—STAND PIPES.—XV. THE CONNECTION OF SETTLING RESERVOIRS, FILTER BEDS AND SERVICE RESERVOIRS.—XVI. PUMPING MACHINERY.—XVII. FLOW OF WATER IN CONDUITS—PIPES AND OPEN CHANNELS.—XVIII. DISTRIBUTION SYSTEMS.—XIX. SPECIAL PROVISIONS FOR THE EXTINCTION OF FIRE.—XX. PIPES FOR WATER-WORKS.—XXI. PREVENTION OF WASTE OF WATER.—XXII. VARIOUS APPLIANCES USED IN CONNECTION WITH WATER-WORKS.
APPENDIX I. By PROF. JOHN MILNE, F.R.S.—CONSIDERATIONS CONCERNING THE PROBABLE EFFECTS OF EARTHQUAKES ON WATER-WORKS, AND THE SPECIAL PRECAUTIONS TO BE TAKEN IN EARTHQUAKE COUNTRIES.
APPENDIX II. By JOHN DE RIJKE, C.E.—ON SAND DUNES AND DUNE SAND AS A SOURCE OF WATER SUPPLY.

"The chapter upon filtration of water is very complete, and the details of construction well illustrated. . . . The work should be specially valuable to civil engineers engaged in work in Japan, but the interest is by no means confined to that locality."—*Engineer.*

"We congratulate the author upon the practical commonsense shown in the preparation of this work. . . . The plates and diagrams have evidently been prepared with great care, and cannot fail to be of great assistance to the student."—*Builder.*

RURAL WATER SUPPLY.

A Practical Handbook on the Supply of Water and Construction of Water-works for small Country Districts. By ALLAN GREENWELL, A.M.I.C.E., and W. T. CURRY, A.M.I.C.E., F.G.S. With Illustrations. Second Edition, Revised. Crown 8vo, cloth **5/0**

"We conscientiously recommend it as a very useful book for those concerned in obtaining water for small districts, giving a great deal of practical information in a small compass."—*Builder.*
"The volume contains valuable information upon all matters connected with water supply. . . . It is full of details on points which are continually before water-works engineers."—*Nature.*

THE WATER SUPPLY OF CITIES AND TOWNS.

By WILLIAM HUMBER, A. M. Inst. C.E., and M. Inst. M.E., Author of "Cast and Wrought Iron Bridge Construction," &c., &c. Illustrated with 50 Double Plates, 1 Single Plate, Coloured Frontispiece, and upwards of 250 Woodcuts, and containing 400 pp. of Text. Imp. 4to, elegantly and substantially half-bound in morocco . . . . *Net* **£6 6s.**

LIST OF CONTENTS. I. HISTORICAL SKETCH OF SOME OF THE MEANS THAT HAVE BEEN ADOPTED FOR THE SUPPLY OF WATER TO CITIES AND TOWNS.—II. WATER AND THE FOREIGN MATTER USUALLY ASSOCIATED WITH IT.—III. RAINFALL AND EVAPORATION.—IV. SPRINGS AND THE WATER-BEARING FORMATIONS OF VARIOUS DISTRICTS. —V. MEASUREMENT AND ESTIMATION OF THE FLOW OF WATER.—VI. ON THE SELECTION OF THE SOURCE OF SUPPLY.—VII. WELLS.—VIII. RESERVOIRS.—IX. THE PURIFICATION OF WATER.—X. PUMPS.—XI. PUMPING MACHINERY.—XII. CONDUITS.—XIII. DISTRIBUTION OF WATER.—XIV. METERS, SERVICE PIPES, AND HOUSE FITTINGS.—XV. THE LAW AND ECONOMY OF WATER-WORKS.—XVI. CONSTANT AND INTERMITTENT SUPPLY.— XVII. DESCRIPTION OF PLATES.—APPENDICES, GIVING TABLES OF RATES OF SUPPLY, VELOCITIES, &c., &c., TOGETHER WITH SPECIFICATIONS OF SEVERAL WORKS ILLUSTRATED, AMONG WHICH WILL BE FOUND: ABERDEEN, BIDEFORD, CANTERBURY, DUNDEE, HALIFAX, LAMBETH, ROTHERHAM, DUBLIN, AND OTHERS.

"The most systematic and valuable work upon water supply hitherto produced in English, or in any other language. Mr. Humber's work is characterised almost throughout by an exhaustiveness much more distinctive of French and German than of English technical treatises." —*Engineer.*

THE PROGRESS OF ENGINEERING (1863-6).

By WM. HUMBER, A.M.Inst.C.E. Complete in Four Vols. Containing 148 Double Plates, with Portraits and Copious Descriptive Letterpress. Impl. 4to, half-morocco. Price, complete, **£12 12s.** ; or each Volume sold separately at **£3 3s.** per Volume. *Descriptive List of Contents on application.*

HYDRAULIC POWER ENGINEERING.

A Practical Manual on the Concentration and Transmission of Power by Hydraulic Machinery. By G. CROYDON MARKS, A.M. Inst. C.E. With nearly 200 Illustrations. 8vo, cloth.   *Net* **9/0**

SUMMARY OF CONTENTS. PRINCIPLES OF HYDRAULICS.—THE FLOW OF WATER. —HYDRAULIC PRESSURES, MATERIAL.—TEST LOAD PACKINGS FOR SLIDING SURFACES. —PIPE JOINTS.—CONTROLLING VALVES.—PLATFORM LIFTS.—WORKSHOP AND FOUNDRY CRANES.—WAREHOUSE AND DOCK CRANES.—HYDRAULIC ACCUMULATORS.—PRESSES FOR BALING AND OTHER PURPOSES.—SHEET METAL WORKING AND FORGING MACHINERY. —HYDRAULIC RIVETTERS.—HAND, POWER, AND STEAM PUMPS.—TURBINES.—IMPULSE TURBINES.—REACTION TURBINES.—DESIGN OF TURBINES IN DETAIL.—WATER WHEELS. —HYDRAULIC ENGINES.—RECENT ACHIEVEMENTS.—PRESSURE OF WATER.—ACTION OF PUMPS, &c.

"We have nothing but praise for this thoroughly valuable work. The author has succeeded in rendering his subject interesting as well as instructive."—*Practical Engineer.*
"Can be unhesitatingly recommended as a useful and up-to-date manual on hydraulic transmission and utilisation of power."—*Mechanical World*

HYDRAULIC TABLES, CO-EFFICIENTS, & FORMULÆ.

For Finding the Discharge of Water from Orifices, Notches, Weirs, Pipes, and Rivers. With New Formulæ, Tables, and General Information on Rain-fall, Catchment-Basins, Drainage, Sewerage, Water Supply for Towns and Mill Power. By JOHN NEVILLE, C.E., M.R.I.A. Third Edition, revised, with additions. Numerous Illustrations. Crown 8vo, cloth . . . **14/0**

"It is, of all English books on the subject, the one nearest to completeness."—*Architect.*

HYDRAULIC MANUAL.

Consisting of Working Tables and Explanatory Text. Intended as a Guide in Hydraulic Calculations and Field Operations. By LEWIS D'A. JACKSON, Author of "Aid to Survey Practice," "Modern Metrology," &c. Fourth Edition, Enlarged. Large crown 8vo, cloth **16/0**

"The author has constructed a manual which may be accepted as a trustworthy guide to this branch of the engineer's profession."—*Engineering.*

WATER ENGINEERING.

A Practical Treatise on the Measurement, Storage, Conveyance, and Utilisation of Water for the Supply of Towns, for Mill Power, and for other Purposes. By CHARLES SLAGG, A. M. Inst. C.E. Second Edition. Crown 8vo, cloth . **7/6**

"As a small practical treatise on the water supply of towns, and on some applications of water-power, the work is in many respects excellent."—*Engineering.*

THE RECLAMATION OF LAND FROM TIDAL WATERS.

A Handbook for Engineers, Landed Proprietors, and others interested in Works of Reclamation. By ALEX. BEAZELEV, M.Inst. C.E.   8vo, cloth.

Net **10/6**

" The book shows in a concise way what has to be done in reclaiming land from the sea, and the best way of doing it. The work contains a great deal of practical and useful information which cannot fail to be of service to engineers entrusted with the enclosure of salt marshes, and to land-owners intending to reclaim land from the sea."—*The Engineer.*

" The author has carried out his task efficiently and well, and his book contains a large amount of information of great service to engineers and others interested in works of reclamation." —*Nature.*

MASONRY DAMS FROM INCEPTION TO COMPLETION.

Including numerous Formulæ, Forms of Specification and Tender, Pocket Diagram of Forces, &c. For the use of Civil and Mining Engineers. By C. F. COURTNEY, M. Inst. C.E.   8vo, cloth **9/0**

" The volume contains a good deal of valuable data. Many useful suggestions will be found in the remarks on site and position, location of dam, foundations and construction."—*Building News.*

RIVER BARS.

The Causes of their Formation, and their Treatment by "Induced Tidal Scour"; with a Description of the Successful Reduction by this Method of the Bar at Dublin. By I. J. MANN, Assist. Eng. to the Dublin Port and Docks Board. Royal 8vo, cloth **7/6**

" We recommend all interested in harbour works—and, indeed, those concerned in the improvements of rivers generally—to read Mr. Mann's interesting work."—*Engineer.*

TRAMWAYS: THEIR CONSTRUCTION AND WORKING.

Embracing a Comprehensive History of the System; with an exhaustive Analysis of the Various Modes of Traction, including Horse Power, Steam, Cable Traction, Electric Traction, &c.; a Description of the Varieties of Rolling Stock; and ample Details of Cost and Working Expenses. New Edition, Thoroughly Revised, and Including the Progress recently made in Tramway Construction, &c., &c. By D. KINNEAR CLARK, M. Inst. C.E. With 400 Illustrations. 8vo, 780 pp., buckram.   **28/0**

" The new volume is one which will rank, among tramway engineers and those interested in tramway working, with the Author's world-famed book on railway machinery."—*The Engineer.*

SURVEYING AS PRACTISED BY CIVIL ENGINEERS AND SURVEYORS.

Including the Setting-out of Works for Construction and Surveys Abroad, with many Examples taken from Actual Practice. A Handbook for use in the Field and the Office, intended also as a Text-book for Students. By JOHN WHITE-LAW, Jun., A.M. Inst. C.E., Author of "Points and Crossings." With about 260 Illustrations. Demy 8vo, cloth . . . . . . *Net* **10/6**

" This work is written with admirable lucidity, and will certainly be found of distinct value both to students and to those engaged in actual practice."—*The Builder.*

PRACTICAL SURVEYING.

A Text-Book for Students preparing for Examinations or for Survey-work in the Colonies. By GEORGE W. USILL, A.M.I.C.E. With 4 Lithographic Plates and upwards of 330 Illustrations. Seventh Edition. Including Tables of Natural Sines, Tangents, Secants, &c. Crown 8vo, **7/6** cloth; or, on THIN PAPER, leather, gilt edges, rounded corners, for pocket use . . . **12/6**

" The best forms of instruments are described as to their construction, uses and modes of employment, and there are innumerable hints on work and equipment such as the author, in his experience as surveyor, draughtsman and teacher, has found necessary, and which the student in his inexperience will find most serviceable."—*Engineer.*

" The first book which should be put in the hands of a pupil of Civil Engineering."— *Architect.*

AID TO SURVEY PRACTICE.

For Reference in Surveying, Levelling, and Setting-out; and in Route Sur-veys of Travellers by Land and Sea. With Tables, Illustrations, and Records. By LOWIS D'A. JACKSON, A.M.I.C.E. Second Edition, Enlarged. 8vo, cloth **12/6**

" Mr. Jackson has produced a valuable *vade-mecum* for the surveyor. We can recommend this book as containing an admirable supplement to the teaching of the accomplished surveyor."— *Athenæum.*

" The author brings to his work a fortunate union of theory and practical experience which, aided by a clear and lucid style of writing, renders the book a very useful one."—*Builder.*

SURVEYING WITH THE TACHEOMETER.

A practical Manual for the use of Civil and Military Engineers and Surveyors. Including two series of Tables specially computed for the Reduction of Readings in Sexagesimal and in Centesimal Degrees. By NEIL KENNEDY, M. Inst. C.E. With Diagrams and Plates. Demy 8vo, cloth.   *Net* **10/6**

" The work is very clearly written, and should remove all difficulties in the way of any surveyor desirous of making use of this useful and rapid instrument."—*Nature.*

ENGINEER'S & MINING SURVEYOR'S FIELD BOOK.

Consisting of a Series of Tables, with Rules, Explanations of Systems, and use of Theodolite for Traverse Surveying and plotting the work with minute accuracy by means of Straight Edge and Set Square only ; Levelling with the Theodolite, Setting-out Curves with and without the Theodolite, Earthwork Tables, &c. By W. DAVIS HASKOLL, C.E. With numerous Woodcuts. Fourth Edition, Enlarged. Crown 8vo, cloth **12/0**

" The book is very handy ; the separate tables of sines and tangents to every minute will make it useful for many other purposes, the genuine traverse tables existing all the same."—*Athenæum.*

LAND AND MARINE SURVEYING.

In Reference to the Preparation of Plans for Roads and Railways ; Canals, Rivers, Towns' Water Supplies ; Docks and Harbours. With Description and Use of Surveying Instruments. By W. DAVIS HASKOLL, C.E. Second Edition, Revised, with Additions. Large crown 8vo, cloth . . . **9/0**

" This book must prove of great value to the student. We have no hesitation in recommending it, feeling assured that it will more than repay a careful study."—*Mechanical World.*
" A most useful book for the student. We can strongly recommend it as a carefully-written and valuable text-book. It enjoys a well-deserved repute among surveyors."—*Builder.*

PRINCIPLES AND PRACTICE OF LEVELLING.

Showing its Application to Purposes of Railway and Civil Engineering in the Construction of Roads ; with Mr. TELFORD'S Rules for the same. By FREDERICK W. SIMMS, M. Inst. C.E. Eighth Edition, with LAW'S Practical Examples for Setting-out Railway Curves, and TRAUTWINE'S Field Practice of Laying-out Circular Curves. With 7 Plates and numerous Woodcuts. 8vo **8/6**

" The text-book on levelling in most of our engineering schools and colleges."—*Engineer.*
" The publishers have rendered a substantial service to the profession, especially to the younger members, by bringing out the present edition of Mr. Simms's useful work."—*Engineering.*

AN OUTLINE OF THE METHOD OF CONDUCTING A TRIGONOMETRICAL SURVEY.

For the Formation of Geographical and Topographical Maps and Plans, Military Reconnaissance, LEVELLING, &c., with Useful Problems, Formulæ, and Tables. By Lieut.-General FROME, R.E. Fourth Edition, Revised and partly Re-written by Major-General Sir CHARLES WARREN, G.C.M.G., R.E. With 19 Plates and 115 Woodcuts, royal 8vo, cloth **16/0**

" No words of praise from us can strengthen the position so well and so steadily maintained by this work. Sir Charles Warren has revised the entire work, and made such additions as were necessary to bring every portion of the contents up to the present date."—*Broad Arrow.*

TABLES OF TANGENTIAL ANGLES AND MULTIPLES FOR SETTING-OUT CURVES.

From 5 to 200 Radius. By A. BEAZELEY, M. Inst. C.E. 6th Edition, Revised. With an Appendix on the use of the Tables for Measuring up Curves. Printed on 50 Cards, and sold in a cloth box, waistcoat-pocket size. **3/6**

" Each table is printed on a small card, which, placed on the theodolite, leaves the hands free to manipulate the instrument—no small advantage as regards the rapidity of work."—*Engineer.*
" Very handy : a man may know that all his day's work must fall on two of these cards, which he puts into his own card-case, and leaves the rest behind."—*Athenæum.*

HANDY GENERAL EARTH-WORK TABLES.

Giving the Contents in Cubic Yards of Centre and Slopes of Cuttings and Embankments from 3 inches to 80 feet in Depth or Height, for use with either 66 feet Chain or 100 feet Chain. By J. H. WATSON BUCK, M. Inst. C.E. On a Sheet mounted in cloth case **3/6**

EARTHWORK TABLES.

Showing the Contents in Cubic Yards of Embankments, Cuttings, &c., of Heights or Depths up to an average of 80 feet. By JOSEPH BROADBENT, C.E., and FRANCIS CAMPIN, C.E. Crown 8vo, cloth **5/0**

"The way in which accuracy is attained, by a simple division of each cross section into three elements, two in which are constant and one variable, is ingenious."—*Athenæum.*

A MANUAL ON EARTHWORK.

By ALEX. J. GRAHAM, C.E. With numerous Diagrams. Second Edition. 18mo, cloth **2/6**

THE CONSTRUCTION OF LARGE TUNNEL SHAFTS.

A Practical and Theoretical Essay. By J. H. WATSON BUCK, M. Inst. C.E., Resident Engineer, L. and N. W. R. With Folding Plates, 8vo, cloth **12/0**

"Many of the methods given are of extreme practical value to the mason, and the observations on the form of arch, the rules for ordering the stone, and the construction of the templates, will be found of considerable use. We commend the book to the engineering profession."—*Building News.*

"Will be regarded by civil engineers as of the utmost value, and calculated to save much time and obviate many mistakes."—*Colliery Guardian.*

CAST & WROUGHT IRON BRIDGE CONSTRUCTION

(A Complete and Practical Treatise on), including Iron Foundations. In Three Parts.—Theoretical, Practical, and Descriptive. By WILLIAM HUMBER, A. M. Inst. C.E., and M. Inst. M.E. Third Edition, revised and much improved, with 115 Double Plates (20 of which now first appear in this edition), and numerous Additions to the Text. In 2 vols., imp. 4to, half-bound in morocco . . . . **£6 16s. 6D.**

"A very valuable contribution to the standard literature of civil engineering. In addition to elevations, plans, and sections, large scale details are given, which very much enhance the instructive worth of those illustrations."—*Civil Engineer and Architect's Journal.*

"Mr. Humber's stately volumes, lately issued—in which the most important bridges erected during the last five years, under the direction of the late Mr. Brunel, Sir W. Cubitt, Mr. Hawkshaw, Mr. Page, Mr. Fowler, Mr. Hemans, and others among our most eminent engineers, are drawn and specified in great detail."—*Engineer.*

ESSAY ON OBLIQUE BRIDGES

(Practical and Theoretical). With 13 large Plates. By the late GEORGE WATSON BUCK, M.I.C.E. Fourth Edition, revised by his Son, J. H. WATSON BUCK, M.I.C.E.; and with the addition of Description to Diagrams for Facilitating the Construction of Oblique Bridges, by W. H. BARLOW, M.I.C.E. Royal 8vo, cloth **12/0**

"The standard text-book for all engineers regarding skew arches is Mr. Buck's treatise, and it would be impossible to consult a better."—*Engineer.*

"Mr. Buck's treatise is recognised as a standard text-book, and his treatment has divested the subject of many of the intricacies supposed to belong to it. As a guide to the engineer and architect, on a confessedly difficult subject, Mr. Buck's work is unsurpassed."—*Building News.*

THE CONSTRUCTION OF OBLIQUE ARCHES

(A Practical Treatise on). By JOHN HART. Third Edition, with Plates. Imperial 8vo, cloth **8/0**

GRAPHIC AND ANALYTIC STATICS.

In their Practical Application to the Treatment of Stresses in Roofs Solid Girders, Lattice, Bowstring, and Suspension Bridges, Braced Iron Arches and Piers, and other Frameworks. By R. HUDSON GRAHAM, C.E. Containing Diagrams and Plates to Scale. With numerous Examples, many taken from existing Structures. Specially arranged for Class-work in Colleges and Universities. Second Edition, Revised and Enlarged. 8vo, cloth . **16/0**

"Mr. Graham's book will find a place wherever graphic and analytic statics are used or studied."—*Engineer.*

"The work is excellent from a practical point of view, and has evidently been prepared with much care. The directions for working are ample, and are illustrated by an abundance of well-selected examples. It is an excellent text-book for the practical draughtsman."—*Athenæum.*

WEIGHTS OF WROUGHT IRON & STEEL GIRDERS.

A Graphic Table for Facilitating the Computation of the Weights of Wrought Iron and Steel Girders, &c., for Parliamentary and other Estimates. By J. H. WATSON BUCK, M. Inst. C.E. On a Sheet **2/6**

GEOMETRY FOR TECHNICAL STUDENTS.

An Introduction to Pure and Applied Geometry and the Mensuration of Surfaces and Solids, including Problems in Plane Geometry useful in Drawing. By E. H. SPRAGUE, A.M.I.C.E. Crown 8vo, cloth. [*Just Published.* *Net* 1/0

PRACTICAL GEOMETRY.

For the Architect, Engineer, and Mechanic. Giving Rules for the Delineation and Application of various Geometrical Lines, Figures, and Curves. By E. W. TARN, M.A., Architect. 8vo, cloth **9/0**

" No book with the same objects in view has ever been published in which the clearness of the rules laid down and the illustrative diagrams have been so satisfactory."—*Scotsman.*

THE GEOMETRY OF COMPASSES.

Or, Problems Resolved by the mere Description of Circles and the Use of Coloured Diagrams and Symbols. By OLIVER BYRNE. Coloured Plates. Crown 8vo, cloth **3/6**

EXPERIMENTS ON THE FLEXURE OF BEAMS

Resulting in the Discovery of New Laws of Failure by Buckling. By ALBERT E. GUY. Medium 8vo, cloth. [*Just Published.* Net **9/0**

HANDY BOOK FOR THE CALCULATION OF STRAINS

In Girders and Similar Structures and their Strength. Consisting of Formulæ and Corresponding Diagrams, with numerous details for Practical Application, &c. By WILLIAM HUMBER, A. M. Inst. C.E., &c. Fifth Edition. Crown 8vo, with nearly 100 Woodcuts and 3 Plates, cloth . . . **7/6**

" The formulæ are neatly expressed, and the diagrams good."—*Athenæum.*
" We heartily commend this really *handy* book to our engineer and architect readers."—*English Mechanic.*

TRUSSES OF WOOD AND IRON.

Practical Applications of Science in Determining the Stresses, Breaking Weights, Safe Loads, Scantlings, and Details of Construction. With Complete Working Drawings. By WILLIAM GRIFFITHS, Surveyor. 8vo, cloth **4/6**

" This handy little book enters so minutely into every detail connected with the construction of roof trusses that no student need be ignorant of these matters."—*Practical Engineer.*

THE STRAINS ON STRUCTURES OF IRONWORK.

With Practical Remarks on Iron Construction. By F. W. SHEILDS, M.I.C.E. 8vo, cloth **5/0**

A TREATISE ON THE STRENGTH OF MATERIALS.

With Rules for Application in Architecture, the Construction of Suspension Bridges, Railways, &c. By PETER BARLOW, F.R.S. A new Edition, revised by his Sons, P. W. BARLOW, F.R.S., and W. H. BARLOW, F.R.S. ; to which are added, Experiments by HODGKINSON, FAIRBAIRN, and KIRKALDY; and Formulæ for calculating Girders, &c. Edited by WM. HUMBER, A.M.I.C.E. 8vo, 400 pp., with 19 Plates and numerous Woodcuts, cloth . . **18/0**

" Valuable alike to the student, tyro, and the experienced practitioner, it will always rank n future as it has hitherto done, as the standard treatise on that particular subject."—*Engineer.*

SAFE RAILWAY WORKING.

A Treatise on Railway Accidents, their Cause and Prevention ; with a Description of Modern Appliances and Systems. By CLEMENT E. STRETTON, C.E. With Illustrations and Coloured Plates. Third Edition, Enlarged. Crown 8vo, cloth **3/6**

" A book for the engineer, the directors, the managers; and, in short, all who wish for information on railway matters will find a perfect encyclopædia in 'Safe Railway Working.'"—*Railway Review.*

EXPANSION OF STRUCTURES BY HEAT.

By JOHN KEILY, C.E., late of the Indian Public Works Department. Crown 8vo, cloth **3/6**

" The aim the author has set before him, viz., to show the effects of heat upon metallic and other structures, is a laudable one, for this is a branch of physics upon which the engineer or architect can find but little reliable and comprehensive data in books."—*Builder.*

PUBLICATIONS OF THE ENGINEERING
STANDARDS COMMITTEE.

THE ENGINEERING STANDARDS COMMITTEE is the outcome of a Committee appointed by the Institution of Civil Engineers at the instance of Sir John Wolfe Barry, K.C.B., to inquire into the advisability of Standardising Rolled Iron and Steel Sections.

The Committee is supported by the Institution of Civil Engineers, the Institution of Mechanical Engineers, the Institution of Naval Architects, the Iron and Steel Institute, and the Institution of Electrical Engineers ; and the value and importance of its labours has been emphatically recognised by his Majesty's Government, who have made a liberal grant from the Public Funds by way of contribution to the financial resources of the Committee.

The subjects already dealt with, or under consideration by the Committee, include not only Rolled Iron and Steel Sections, but Tests for Iron and Steel Material used in the Construction of Ships and their Machinery, Bridges and General Building Construction, Railway Rolling Stock Underframes, Component Parts of Locomotives, Railway and Tramway Rails, Electrical Plant, Insulating Materials, Screw Threads and Limit Gauges, Pipe Flanges, Cement, &c.

Reports already Published :—

1. **BRITISH STANDARD SECTIONS.**

    List 1. EQUAL ANGLES.—List 2. UNEQUAL ANGLES.—List 3. BULB ANGLES. List 4. BULB TEES.—List 5. BULB PLATES.—List 7. CHANNELS.—List 8. BEAMS. F'cap. folio, sewed.   [*Just Published. Net* **1 0**

2. **BRITISH STANDARD TRAMWAY RAILS AND FISH PLATES : STANDARD SECTIONS AND SPECIFICATION.**

    F'cap. folio, sewed.   [*Just Published. Net* **21 0**

3. **REPORT ON THE INFLUENCE OF GAUGE LENGTH AND SECTION OF TEST BAR ON THE PERCENTAGE OF ELONGATION.**

    By Professor W. C. UNWIN, F.R.S. F'cap. folio, sewed.
    [*Just Published. Net* **2 6**

4. **PROPERTIES OF STANDARD BEAMS.**

    Demy 8vo, sewed.   [*Just Published. Net* **1 0**

MARINE ENGINEERING, SHIPBUILDING, NAVIGATION, ETC.

THE NAVAL ARCHITECT'S AND SHIPBUILDER'S

POCKET-BOOK of Formulæ, Rules, and Tables, and Marine Engineer's and Surveyor's Handy Book of Reference. By CLEMENT MACKROW, M.I.N.A. Eighth Edition, Carefully Revised and Enlarged. Fcap., leather. *Net* 12/6

SUMMARY OF CONTENTS:—SIGNS AND SYMBOLS, DECIMAL FRACTIONS.—TRIGONOMETRY.—PRACTICAL GEOMETRY.—MENSURATION.—CENTRES AND MOMENTS OF FIGURES.—MOMENTS OF INERTIA AND RADII OF GYRATION.—ALGEBRAICAL EXPRESSIONS FOR SIMPSON'S RULES.—MECHANICAL PRINCIPLES.—CENTRE OF GRAVITY.—LAWS OF MOTION.—DISPLACEMENT, CENTRE OF BUOYANCY.—CENTRE OF GRAVITY OF SHIP'S HULL.—STABILITY CURVES AND METACENTRES.—SEA AND SHALLOW-WATER WAVES.—ROLLING OF SHIPS.—PROPULSION AND RESISTANCE OF VESSELS.—SPEED TRIALS.—SAILING CENTRE OF EFFORT.—DISTANCES DOWN RIVERS, COAST LINES.—STEERING AND RUDDERS OF VESSELS.—LAUNCHING CALCULATIONS AND VELOCITIES.—WEIGHT OF MATERIAL AND GEAR.—GUN PARTICULARS AND WEIGHT.—STANDARD GAUGES.—RIVETED JOINTS AND RIVETING.—STRENGTH AND TESTS OF MATERIALS.—BINDING AND SHEARING STRESSES, &c.—STRENGTH OF SHAFTING, PILLARS, WHEELS, &c.—HYDRAULIC DATA, &c.—CONIC SECTIONS, CATENARIAN CURVES.—MECHANICAL POWERS, WORK.—BOARD OF TRADE REGULATIONS FOR BOILERS AND ENGINES.—BOARD OF TRADE REGULATIONS FOR SHIPS.—LLOYD'S RULES FOR BOILERS.—LLOYD'S WEIGHT OF CHAINS.—LLOYD'S SCANTLINGS FOR SHIPS.—DATA OF ENGINES AND VESSELS.—SHIPS' FITTINGS AND TESTS.—SEASONING PRESERVING TIMBER.—MEASUREMENT OF TIMBER.—ALLOYS, PAINTS, VARNISHES.—DATA FOR STOWAGE.—ADMIRALTY TRANSPORT REGULATIONS.—RULES FOR HORSE-POWER, SCREW PROPELLERS, &c.—PERCENTAGES FOR BUTT STRAPS, &c.—PARTICULARS OF YACHTS.—MASTING AND RIGGING VESSELS.—DISTANCES OF FOREIGN PORTS.—TONNAGE TABLES.—VOCABULARY OF FRENCH AND ENGLISH TERMS.—ENGLISH WEIGHTS AND MEASURES.—FOREIGN WEIGHTS AND MEASURES.—DECIMAL EQUIVALENTS.—FOREIGN MONEY.—DISCOUNT AND WAGES TABLES.—USEFUL NUMBERS AND READY RECKONERS.—TABLES OF CIRCULAR MEASURES.—TABLES OF AREAS OF AND CIRCUMFERENCES OF CIRCLES.—TABLES OF AREAS OF SEGMENTS OF CIRCLES.—TABLES OF SQUARES AND CUBES AND ROOTS OF NUMBERS.—TABLES OF LOGARITHMS OF NUMBERS.—TABLES OF HYPERBOLIC LOGARITHMS.—TABLES OF NATURAL SINES, TANGENTS, &c.—TABLES OF LOGARITHMIC SINES, TANGENTS, &c.

"In these days of advanced knowledge a work like this is of the greatest value. It contains a vast amount of information. We unhesitatingly say that it is the most valuable compilation for its specific purpose that has ever been printed. No naval architect, engineer, surveyor, seaman, wood or iron shipbuilder, can afford to be without this work."—*Nautical Magazine.*

"Should be used by all who are engaged in the construction or design of vessels. . . . Will be found to contain the most useful tables and formulæ required by shipbuilders, carefully collected from the best authorities, and put together in a popular and simple form. The book is one of exceptional merit."—*Engineer.*

"The professional shipbuilder has now, in a convenient and accessible form, reliable data for solving many of the numerous problems that present themselves in the course of his work."—*Iron.*

"There is no doubt that a pocket-book of this description must be a necessity in the shipbuilding trade. . . The volume contains a mass of useful information clearly expressed and presented in a handy form."—*Marine Engineer.*

WANNAN'S MARINE ENGINEER'S GUIDE

To Board of Trade Examinations for Certificates of Competency. Containing all Latest Questions to Date, with Simple, Clear, and Correct Solutions ; 302 Elementary Questions with Illustrated Answers, and Verbal Questions and Answers ; complete Set of Drawings with Statements completed. By A. C. WANNAN, C.E., Consulting Engineer, and E. W. I. WANNAN, M.I.M.E., Certificated First Class Marine Engineer. With numerous Engravings. Third Edition, Enlarged. 500 pages. Large crown 8vo, cloth . . *Net* 10/6

"The book is clearly and plainly written and avoids unnecessary explanations and formulas, and we consider it a valuable book for students of marine engineering."—*Nautical Magazine.*

WANNAN'S MARINE ENGINEER'S POCKET-BOOK.

Containing Latest Board of Trade Rules and Data for Marine Engineers. By A. C. WANNAN. Third Edition, Revised, Enlarged, and Brought up to Date. Square 18mo, with thumb Index, leather. [*Just Published.* 5/0

"There is a great deal of useful information in this little pocket-book. It is of the rule-of thumb order, and is, on that account, well adapted to the uses of the sea-going engineer."—*Engineer.*

THE SHIPBUILDING INDUSTRY OF GERMANY.

Compiled and Edited by G. LEHMANN-FELSKOWSKI. With Coloured Prints, Art Supplements, and numerous Illustrations throughout the text. Super-royal 4to, cloth. [*Just Published.* *Net* 10/6

SEA TERMS, PHRASES, AND WORDS

(Technical Dictionary of) used in the English and French Languages (English-French, French-English). For the Use of Seamen, Engineers, Pilots, Shipbuilders, Shipowners, and Ship-brokers. Compiled by W. PIRRIE, late of the African Steamship Company. Fcap. 8vo, cloth limp . . . **5/0**

" This volume will be highly appreciated by seamen, engineers, pilots, shipbuilders and ship-owners. It will be found wonderfully accurate and complete."—*Scotsman.*

" A very useful dictionary, which has long been wanted by French and English engineers, masters, officers and others."—*Shipping World.*

ELECTRIC SHIP-LIGHTING.

A Handbook on the Practical Fitting and Running of Ships' Electrical Plant, for the Use of Shipowners and Builders, Marine Electricians and Sea-going Engineers in Charge. By J. W. URQUHART, Author of "Electric Light," "Dynamo Construction," &c. Second Edition, Revised and Extended. With numerous Illustrations. Crown 8vo, cloth **7/6**

MARINE ENGINEER'S POCKET-BOOK.

Consisting of useful Tables and Formulæ. By FRANK PROCTOR, A.I.N.A. Third Edition. Royal 32mo, leather. **4/0**

" We recommend it to our readers as going far to supply a long-felt want."—*Naval Science.*
" A most useful companion to all marine engineers."—*United Service Gazette.*

ELEMENTARY MARINE ENGINEERING.

A Manual for Young Marine Engineers and Apprentices. In the Form of Questions and Answers on Metals, Alloys, Strength of Materials, Construction and Management of Marine Engines and Boilers, Geometry, &c. With an Appendix of Useful Tables. By J. S. BREWER. Crown 8vo, cloth **1/6**

"Contains much valuable information for the class for whom it is intended, especially in the chapters on the management of boilers and engines."—*Nautical Magazine.*

MARINE ENGINES AND STEAM VESSELS.

A Treatise on. By ROBERT MURRAY, C.E. Eighth Edition, thoroughly Revised, with considerable Additions by the Author and by GEORGE CARLISLE, C.E., Senior Surveyor to the Board of Trade at Liverpool. Crown 8vo, cloth **4/6**

PRACTICAL NAVIGATION.

Consisting of THE SAILOR'S SEA-BOOK, by JAMES GREENWOOD and W. H. ROSSER; together with the requisite Mathematical and Nautical Tables for the Working of the Problems, by HENRY LAW, C.E., and Professor J. R. YOUNG. Illustrated. 12mo, strongly half-bound **7/0**

THE ART AND SCIENCE OF SAILMAKING.

By SAMUEL B. SADLER, Practical Sailmaker, late in the employment of Messrs. Ratsey and Lapthorne, of Cowes and Gosport. With Plates and other Illustrations. Small 4to, cloth **12/6**

" This extremely practical work gives a complete education in all the branches of the manu-facture, cutting out, roping, seaming, and goring. It is copiously illustrated, and will form a first-rate text-book and guide."—*Portsmouth Times.*

CHAIN CABLES AND CHAINS.

Comprising Sizes and Curves of Links, Studs, &c., Iron for Cables and Chains, Chain Cable and Chain Making, Forming and Welding Links, Strength of Cables and Chains, Certificates for Cables, Marking Cables, Prices of Chain Cables and Chains, Historical Notes, Acts of Parliament, Statutory Tests, Charges for Testing, List of Manufacturers of Cables, &c., &c. By THOMAS W. TRAILL, F.E.R.N., M.Inst.C.E., Engineer-Surveyor-in-Chief, Board of Trade, Inspector of Chain Cable and Anchor Proving Establishments, and General Superintendent Lloyd's Committee on Proving Establishments. With numerous Tables, Illustrations, and Lithographic Drawings. Folio, cloth, bevelled boards . . . . **£2 2s.**

" It contains a vast amount of valuable information. Nothing seems to be wanting to make it a complete and standard work of reference on the subject."—*Nautical Magazine.*

MINING, METALLURGY, AND COLLIERY WORKING.

THE OIL FIELDS OF RUSSIA AND THE RUSSIAN PETROLEUM INDUSTRY.

A Practical Handbook on the Exploration, Exploitation, and Management of Russian Oil Properties, including Notes on the Origin of Petroleum in Russia, a Description of the Theory and Practice of Liquid Fuel, and a Translation of the Rules and Regulations concerning Russian Oil Properties. By A. BEEBY THOMPSON, A.M.I.M.E., late Chief Engineer and Manager of the European Petroleum Company's Russian Oil Properties. About 500 pp. With numerous Illustrations and Photographic Plates, and a Map of the Balakhany-Saboontchy-Romany Oil Field. Super-royal 8vo, cloth.

[Just Published. Net **£3 3s.**

MACHINERY FOR METALLIFEROUS MINES.

A Practical Treatise for Mining Engineers, Metallurgists, and Managers of Mines. By E. HENRY DAVIES, M.E., F.G.S. 600 pp. With Folding Plates and other Illustrations. Medium 8vo, cloth .   .   .   . Net **25/0**

" Deals exhaustively with the many and complex details which go to make up the sum total of machinery and other requirements for the successful working of metalliferous mines, and as a book of ready reference is of the highest value to mine managers and directors."—*Mining Journal.*

THE DEEP LEVEL MINES OF THE RAND,

And their Future Development, considered from the Commercial Point of View. By G. A. DENNY (of Johannesburg), M.N.E.I.M.E., Consulting Engineer to the General Mining and Finance Corporation, Ltd., of London, Berlin, Paris, and Johannesburg. Fully Illustrated with Diagrams and Folding Plates. Royal 8vo, buckram .   .   .   . Net **25/0**

" Mr. Denny by confining himself to the consideration of the future of the deep-level mines of the Rand breaks new ground, and by dealing with the subject rather from a commercial stand-point than from a scientific one, appeals to a wide circle of readers. The book cannot fail to prove of very great value to investors in South African mines."—*Mining Journal.*

PROSPECTING FOR GOLD.

A Handbook of Information and Hints for Prospectors based on Personal Experience. By DANIEL J. RANKIN, F.R.S.G.S., M.R.A.S., formerly Manager of the Central African Company, and Leader of African Gold Pros-pecting Expeditions. With Illustrations specially Drawn and Engraved for the Work. F'cap. 8vo, leather .   .   .   . Net **7/6**

" This well-compiled book contains a collection of the richest gems of useful knowledge for the prospector's benefit. A special table is given to accelerate the spotting at a glance of minerals associated with gold."—*Mining Journal.*

THE METALLURGY OF GOLD.

A Practical Treatise on the Metallurgical Treatment of Gold-bearing Ores. Including the Assaying, Melting, and Refining of Gold. By M. EISSLER, M. Inst. M.M. Fifth Edition, Enlarged. With over 300 Illustrations and numerous Folding Plates. Medium 8vo, cloth   .   .   . Net **21/0**

" This book thoroughly deserves its title of a 'Practical Treatise.' The whole process of gold mining, from the breaking of the quartz to the assay of the bullion, is described in clear and orderly narrative and with much, but not too much, fulness of detail."—*Saturday Review.*

THE CYANIDE PROCESS OF GOLD EXTRACTION.

And its Practical Application on the Witwatersrand Gold Fields and elsewhere. By M. EISSLER, M. Inst. M.M. With Diagrams and Working Drawings. Third Edition, Revised and Enlarged. 8vo, cloth .   .   .   . Net **7/6**

" This book is just what was needed to acquaint mining men with the actual working of a process which is not only the most popular, but is, as a general rule, the most successful for the extraction of gold from tailings."—*Mining Journal.*

DIAMOND DRILLING FOR GOLD & OTHER MINERALS.

A Practical Handbook on the Use of Modern Diamond Core Drills in Pro-specting and Exploiting Mineral-Bearing Properties, including Particulars of the Costs of Apparatus and Working. By G. A. DENNY, M.N.E. Inst. M.E., M. Inst. M.M. Medium 8vo, 168 pp., with Illustrative Diagrams . **12/6**

" There is certainly scope for a work on diamond drilling, and Mr. Denny deserves grateful recognition for supplying a decided want."—*Mining Journal.*   .

B 2

GOLD ASSAYING.

A Practical Handbook for Assayers, Bankers, Chemists, Bullion Smelters, Goldsmiths, Mining and Metallurgical Engineers, Prospectors, Students, and others. By H. JOSHUA PHILLIPS, F.I.C., F.C.S., A.I.C.E., Author of "Engineering Chemistry," etc. Large Crown 8vo, cloth.
[Just ready, price about **7/6** *net.*

FIELD TESTING FOR GOLD AND SILVER.

A Practical Manual for Prospectors and Miners. By W. H. MERRITT, M.N.E. Inst. M.E., A.R.S.M., &c. With Photographic Plates and other Illustrations. Fcap. 8vo, leather . . . . . . *Net* **5/0**

"As an instructor of prospectors' classes Mr. Merritt has the advantage of knowing exactly the information likely to be most valuable to the miner in the field. The contents cover all the details of sampling and testing gold and silver ores. A useful addition to a prospector's kit."—*Mining Journal.*

THE PROSPECTOR'S HANDBOOK.

A Guide for the Prospector and Traveller in search of Metal-Bearing or other Valuable Minerals. By J. W. ANDERSON, M.A. (Camb.), F.R.G.S. Ninth Edition. Small crown 8vo, **3/6** cloth ; or, leather **4/6**

"Will supply a much-felt want, especially among Colonists, in whose way are so often thrown many mineralogical specimens the value of which it is difficult to determine."—*Engineer.*
"How to find commercial minerals, and how to identify them when they are found, are the leading points to which attention is directed. The author has managed to pack as much practical detail into his pages as would supply material for a book three times its size."—*Mining Journal.*

THE METALLURGY OF SILVER.

A Practical Treatise on the Amalgamation, Roasting, and Lixiviation of Silver Ores. Including the Assaying, Melting, and Refining of Silver Bullion. By M. EISSLER, M. Inst. M.M. Third Edition. Crown 8vo, cloth . **10/6**

"A practical treatise, and a technical work which we are convinced will supply a long-felt want amongst practical men, and at the same time be of value to students and others indirectly connected with the industries."—*Mining Journal.*

THE HYDRO-METALLURGY OF COPPER.

Being an Account of Processes Adopted in the Hydro-Metallurgical Treatment of Cupriferous Ores, Including the Manufacture of Copper Vitriol, with Chapters on the Sources of Supply of Copper and the Roasting of Copper Ores. By M. EISSLER, M. Inst. M.M. 8vo, cloth . . . . *Net* **12/9**

"In this volume the various processes for the extraction of copper by wet methods are fully detailed. Costs are given when available, and a great deal of useful information about the copper industry of the world is presented in an interesting and attractive manner."—*Mining Journal.*

THE METALLURGY OF ARGENTIFEROUS LEAD.

A Practical Treatise on the Smelting of Silver-Lead Ores and the Refining of Lead Bullion. Including Reports on various Smelting Establishments and Descriptions of Modern Smelting Furnaces and Plants in Europe and America. By M. EISSLER, M. Inst. M.M., Author of "The Metallurgy of Gold," &c. Crown 8vo, 400 pp., with 183 Illustrations, cloth **12/6**

"The numerous metallurgical processes, which are fully and extensively treated of, embrace all the stages experienced in the passage of the lead from the various natural states to its issue from the refinery as an article of commerce."—*Practical Engineer.*

METALLIFEROUS MINERALS AND MINING.

By D. C. DAVIES, F.G.S. Sixth Edition, thoroughly Revised and much Enlarged by his Son, E. HENRY DAVIES, M.E., F.G.S. 600 pp., with 173 Illustrations. Large crown 8vo, cloth . . . . . *Net* **12/6**

"Neither the practical miner nor the general reader, interested in mines, can have a better book for his companion and his guide."—*Mining Journal.*

EARTHY AND OTHER MINERALS AND MINING.

By D. C. DAVIES, F.G.S., Author of "Metalliferous Minerals," &c. Third Edition, Revised and Enlarged by his Son, E. HENRY DAVIES, M.E., F.G.S. With about 100 Illustrations. Crown 8vo, cloth **12/6**

"We do not remember to have met with any English work on mining matters that contains the same amount of information packed in equally convenient form."—*Academy.*

BRITISH MINING.

A Treatise on the History, Discovery, Practical Development, and Future Prospects of Metalliferous Mines in the United Kingdom. By ROBERT HUNT, F.R.S., late Keeper of Mining Records. Upwards of 950 pp., with 230 Illustrations. Second Edition, Revised. Super-royal 8vo, cloth **£2 2s.**

POCKET-BOOK FOR MINERS AND METALLURGISTS.

Comprising Rules, Formulæ, Tables, and Notes for Use in Field and Office Work. By F. DANVERS POWER, F.G.S., M.E. Second Edition, Corrected. Fcap. 8vo. leather **9/0**

" This excellent book is an admirable example of its kind, and ought to find a large sale amongst English-speaking prospectors and mining engineers."—*Engineering.*

THE MINER'S HANDBOOK.

A Handy Book of Reference on the subjects of Mineral Deposits, Mining Operations, Ore Dressing, &c. For the Use of Students and others interested in Mining Matters. Compiled by JOHN MILNE, F.R.S., Professor of Mining in the Imperial University of Japan. Third Edition. Fcap. 8vo, leather **7/6**

" Professor Milne's handbook is sure to be received with favour by all connected with mining, and will be extremely popular among students."—*Athenæum.*

IRON ORES of GREAT BRITAIN and IRELAND.

Their Mode of Occurrence, Age and Origin, and the Methods of Searching for and Working Them. With a Notice of some of the Iron Ores of Spain. By J. D. KENDALL, F.G.S., Mining Engineer. Crown 8vo, cloth . . **16/0**

MINE DRAINAGE.

A Complete Practical Treatise on Direct-Acting Underground Steam Pumping Machinery. By STEPHEN MICHELL. Second Edition, Re-written and Enlarged. With 250 Illustrations. Royal 8vo, cloth . *Net* **25/0**

HORIZONTAL PUMPING ENGINES.—ROTARY AND NON-ROTARY HORIZONTAL ENGINES.—SIMPLE AND COMPOUND STEAM PUMPS.—VERTICAL PUMPING ENGINES.— ROTARY AND NON-ROTARY VERTICAL ENGINES.— SIMPLE AND COMPOUND STEAM PUMPS. — TRIPLE-EXPANSION STEAM PUMPS. — PULSATING STEAM PUMPS. — PUMP VALVES.—SINKING PUMPS, &c., &c.

" This volume contains an immense amount of important and interesting new matter. The book should undoubtedly prove of great use to all who wish for information on the subject."—*The Engineer.*

ELECTRICITY AS APPLIED TO MINING.

By ARNOLD LUPTON, M.Inst.C.E., M.I.M.E., M.I.E.E., late Professor of Coal Mining at the Yorkshire College, Victoria University, Mining Engineer and Colliery Manager; G. D. ASPINALL PARR, M.I.E.E., A.M.I.M.E., Associate of the Central Technical College, City and Guilds of London, Head of the Electrical Engineering Department, Yorkshire College, Victoria University; and HERBERT PERKIN, M.I.M.E., Certified Colliery Manager, Assistant Lecturer in the Mining Department of the Yorkshire College, Victoria University. With about 170 Illustrations. Medium 8vo, cloth.
Net **9/0**

(For SUMMARY OF CONTENTS, see page 23.)

THE COLLIERY MANAGER'S HANDBOOK.

A Comprehensive Treatise on the Laying-out and Working of Collieries, Designed as a Book of Reference for Colliery Managers, and for the Use of Coal Mining Students preparing for First-class Certificates. By CALEB PAMELY, Mining Engineer and Surveyor; Member of the North of England Institute of Mining and Mechanical Engineers; and Member of the South Wales Institute of Mining Engineers. With 700 Plans, Diagrams, and other Illustrations. Fourth Edition, Revised and Enlarged. 964 pp. Medium 8vo, cloth **£1 5s.**

GEOLOGY.—SEARCH FOR COAL.—MINERAL LEASES AND OTHER HOLDINGS.— SHAFT SINKING.—FITTING UP THE SHAFT AND SURFACE ARRANGEMENTS.—STEAM BOILERS AND THEIR FITTINGS.—TIMBERING AND WALLING.—NARROW WORK AND METHODS OF WORKING. — UNDERGROUND CONVEYANCE. — DRAINAGE.—THE GASES MET WITH IN MINES; VENTILATION. — ON THE FRICTION OF AIR IN MINES. — THE PRIESTMAN OIL ENGINE; PETROLEUM AND NATURAL GAS. — SURVEYING AND PLANNING.—SAFETY LAMPS AND FIREDAMP DETECTORS.—SUNDRY AND INCIDENTAL OPERATIONS AND APPLIANCES.—COLLIERY EXPLOSIONS.—MISCELLANEOUS QUESTIONS AND ANSWERS.—*Appendix:* SUMMARY OF REPORT OF H.M. COMMISSIONERS ON ACCIDENTS IN MINES.

" Mr. Pamely's work is eminently suited to the purpose or which it is intended, being clear, interesting, exhaustive, rich in detail, and up to date, giving descriptions of the latest machines in every department. A mining engineer could scarcely go wrong who followed this work."—*Colliery Guardian.*

" Mr. Pamely has not only given us a comprehensive reference book of a very high order suitable to the requirements of mining engineers and colliery managers, but has also provided mining students with a class-book that is as interesting as it is instructive."—*Colliery Manager.*

" This is the most complete 'all-round work on coal-mining published in the English language. . . . No library of coal-mining books is complete without it."—*Colliery Engineer* (Scranton, Ba., U.S.A.).

COLLIERY WORKING AND MANAGEMENT.

Comprising the Duties of a Colliery Manager, the Oversight and Arrangement of Labour and Wages, and the different Systems of Working Coal Seams. By H. F. BULMAN and R. A. S. REDMAYNE. 350 pp., with 28 Plates and other Illustrations, including Underground Photographs. Medium 8vo, cloth. **15/0**

"This is, indeed, an admirable Handbook for Colliery Managers, in fact it is an indispensable adjunct to a Colliery Manager's education, as well as being a most useful and interesting work on the subject for all who in any way have to do with coal mining. The underground photographs are an attractive feature of the work, being very lifelike and necessarily true representations of the scenes they depict."—*Colliery Guardian.*

" Mr. Bulman and Mr. Redmayne, who are both experienced Colliery Managers of great literary ability, are to be congratulated on having supplied an authoritative work dealing with a side of the subject of coal mining which has hitherto received but scant treatment. The authors elucidate their text by 119 woodcuts and 28 plates, most of the latter being admirable reproductions of photographs taken underground with the aid of the magnesium flash-light. These illustrations are excellent."—*Nature.*

COAL AND COAL MINING.

By the late Sir WARINGTON W. SMYTH, M.A., F.R.S., Chief Inspector of the Mines of the Crown and of the Duchy of Cornwall. Eighth Edition, Revised and Extended by T. FORSTER BROWN, Mining and Civil Engineer, Chief Inspector of the Mines of the Crown and of the Duchy of Cornwall. Crown 8vo, cloth. **3/6**

" As an outline is given of every known coal-field in this and other countries, as well as of the principal methods of working, the book will doubtless interest a very large number of readers."— *Mining Journal.*

NOTES AND FORMULÆ FOR MINING STUDENTS.

By JOHN HERMAN MERIVALE, M.A., Late Professor of Mining in the Durham College of Science, Newcastle-upon-Tyne. Fourth Edition, Revised and Enlarged. By H. F. BULMAN, A.M.Inst.C.E. Small crown 8vo, cloth. **2/6**

" The author has done his work in a creditable manner, and has produced a book that will be of service to students and those who are practically engaged in mining operations."—*Engineer.*

INFLAMMABLE GAS AND VAPOUR IN THE AIR

(The Detection and Measurement of). By FRANK CLOWES, D.Sc., Lond., F.I.C. With a Chapter on THE DETECTION AND MEASUREMENT OF PETROLEUM VAPOUR by BOVERTON REDWOOD, F.R.S.E., Consulting Adviser to the Corporation of London under the Petroleum Acts. Crown 8vo, cloth. *Net* **5/0**

" Professor Clowes has given us a volume on a subject of much industrial importance . . . Those interested in these matters may be recommended to study this book, which is easy of comprehension and contains many good things."—*The Engineer.*

COAL & IRON INDUSTRIES of the UNITED KINGDOM.

Comprising a Description of the Coal Fields, and of the Principal Seams of Coal, with Returns of their Produce and its Distribution, and Analyses of Special Varieties. Also, an Account of the Occurrence of Iron Ores in Veins or Seams; Analyses of each Variety; and a History of the Rise and Progress of Pig Iron Manufacture. By RICHARD MEADE. 8vo, cloth . . **£1 8s.**

"Of this book we may unreservedly say that it is the best of its class which we have ever met. . . . A book of reference which no one engaged in the iron or coal trades should omit from his library."—*Iron and Coal Trades Review.*

ASBESTOS AND ASBESTIC.

Their Properties, Occurrence, and Use. By ROBERT H. JONES, F.S.A., Mineralogist, Hon. Mem. Asbestos Club, Black Lake, Canada. With Ten Collotype Plates and other Illustrations. Demy 8vo, cloth. . **16/0**

" An interesting and invaluable work."—*Colliery Guardian.*

GRANITES AND OUR GRANITE INDUSTRIES.

By GEORGE F. HARRIS, F.G.S. With Illustrations. Crown 8vo, cloth **2/6**

TRAVERSE TABLES.

For use in Mine Surveying. By WILLIAM LINTERN, C.E. With two plates. Small crown 8vo, cloth . . . . *Net* **3/0**

ELECTRICITY, ELECTRICAL ENGINEERING, ETC.

THE ELEMENTS OF ELECTRICAL ENGINEERING.

A First Year's Course for Students. By TYSON SEWELL, A.I.E.E., Assistant Lecturer and Demonstrator in Electrical Engineering at the Polytechnic, Regent Street, London. Second Edition, Revised, with Additional Chapters on Alternating Current Working, and Appendix of Questions and Answers. 450 pages, with 274 Illustrations. Demy 8vo, cloth. [*Just Published.* Net **7/6**

OHM'S LAW.—UNITS EMPLOYED IN ELECTRICAL ENGINEERING.—SERIES AND PARALLEL CIRCUITS; CURRENT DENSITY AND POTENTIAL DROP IN THE CIRCUIT.—THE HEATING EFFECT OF THE ELECTRIC CURRENT.—THE MAGNETIC EFFECT OF AN ELECTRIC CURRENT.—THE MAGNETISATION OF IRON.—ELECTRO-CHEMISTRY; PRIMARY BATTERIES.—ACCUMULATORS.—INDICATING INSTRUMENTS; AMMETERS, VOLTMETERS, OHMMETERS.—ELECTRICITY SUPPLY METERS.—MEASURING INSTRUMENTS, AND THE MEASUREMENT OF ELECTRICAL RESISTANCE. — MEASUREMENT OF POTENTIAL DIFFERENCE, CAPACITY, CURRENT STRENGTH, AND PERMEABILITY.—ARC LAMPS.—INCANDESCENT LAMPS; MANUFACTURE AND INSTALLATION; PHOTOMETRY. — THE CONTINUOUS CURRENT DYNAMO.—DIRECT CURRENT MOTORS.—ALTERNATING CURRENTS. —TRANSFORMERS, ALTERNATORS, SYNCHRONOUS MOTORS.—POLYPHASE WORKING.—APPENDIX OF QUESTIONS AND ANSWERS.

"An excellent treatise for students of the elementary facts connected with electrical engineering."—*The Electrician.*

"One of the best books for those commencing the study of electrical engineering. Everything is explained in simple language which even a beginner cannot fail to understand."—*Engineer.*

"One welcomes this book, which is sound in its treatment, and admirably calculated to give students the knowledge and information they most require."—*Nature.*

CONDUCTORS FOR ELECTRICAL DISTRIBUTION.

Their Materials and Manufacture, The Calculation of Circuits, Pole-Line Construction, Underground Working, and other Uses. By F. A. C. PERRINE, A.M., D.Sc.; formerly Professor of Electrical Engineering, Leland Stanford, Jr., University; M.Amer.I.E.E. 8vo, cloth. [*Just Published.* Net **20/-**

CONDUCTOR MATERIALS—ALLOYED CONDUCTORS—MANUFACTURE OF WIRE—WIRE-FINISHING—WIRE INSULATION—CABLES—CALCULATION OF CIRCUITS—KELVIN'S LAW OF ECONOMY IN CONDUCTORS—MULTIPLE ARC DISTRIBUTION—ALTERNATING CURRENT CALCULATION—OVERHEAD LINES—POLE LINE—LINE INSULATORS—UNDERGROUND CONDUCTORS.

WIRELESS TELEGRAPHY;

Its Origins, Development, Inventions, and Apparatus. By CHARLES HENRY SEWALL. With 85 Diagrams and Illustrations. Demy 8vo, cloth.

[*Just Published.* Net **10 6**

ARMATURE WINDINGS OF DIRECT CURRENT DYNAMOS.

Extension and Application of a General Winding Rule. By E. ARNOLD, Engineer. Assistant Professor in Electrotechnics and Machine Design at the Riga Polytechnic School. Translated from the Original German by FRANCIS B. DE GRESS, M.E, Chief of Testing Department, Crocker-Wheeler Company. With 146 Illustrations. Medium 8vo, cloth   .   .   . Net **12/-**

ELECTRICITY AS APPLIED TO MINING.

By ARNOLD LUPTON, M.Inst C.E., M.I M.E., M.I.E.E., late Professor of Coal Mining at the Yorkshire College, Victoria University, Mining Engineer and Colliery Manager; G. D. ASPINALL PARR, M.I.E.E., A M.I.M.E., Associate of the Central Technical College, City and Guilds of London, Head of the Electrical Engineering Department, Yorkshire College, Victoria University; and HERBERT PERKIN, M.I.M E. Certificated Colliery Manager, Assistant Lecturer in the Mining Department of the Yorkshire College, Victoria University. With about 170 Illustrations. Medium 8vo, cloth. *Net* **9/-**

INTRODUCTORY. — DYNAMIC ELECTRICITY. — DRIVING OF THE DYNAMO. — THE STEAM TURBINE.—DISTRIBUTION OF ELECTRICAL ENERGY.—STARTING AND STOPPING ELECTRICAL GENERATORS AND MOTORS.—ELECTRIC CABLES.—CENTRAL ELECTRICAL PLANTS.—ELECTRICITY APPLIED TO PUMPING AND HAULING.—ELECTRICITY APPLIED TO COAL-CUTTING.—TYPICAL ELECTRIC PLANTS RECENTLY ERECTED. — ELECTRIC LIGHTING BY ARC AND GLOW LAMPS—MISCELLANEOUS APPLICATIONS OF ELECTRICITY —ELECTRICITY AS COMPARED WITH OTHER MODES OF TRANSMITTING POWER.—DANGERS OF ELECTRICITY.

DYNAMO, MOTOR AND SWITCHBOARD CIRCUITS FOR ELECTRICAL ENGINEERS.

A Practical Handbook dealing with Direct, Alternating and Polyphase Currents. By WILLIAM R. BOWKER, C.E., M.E., E.E., Lecturer on Physics and Electrical Engineering at the Municipal Technical School, Bury. 8vo, cloth. [*Just ready, price about* **6/0** *net.*

DYNAMO ELECTRIC MACHINERY: Its CONSTRUCTION, DESIGN, and OPERATION.

By SAMUEL SHELDON, A.M., Ph.D., Professor of Physics and Electrical Engineering at the Polytechnic Institute of Brooklyn, assisted by HOBART MASON, B.S.

In two volumes, sold separately, as follows :—
Vol. I.—DIRECT CURRENT MACHINES. Third Edition, Revised. Large crown 8vo. 280 pages, with 200 Illustrations . . *Net* **12/0**
Vol. II.—ALTERNATING CURRENT MACHINES. Large crown 8vo. 260 pages, with 184 Illustrations . . . . . *Net* **12/0**
Designed as Text-books for use in Technical Educational Institutions, and by Engineers whose work includes the handling of Direct and Alternating Current Machines respectively, and for Students proficient in mathematics.

ELECTRICAL AND MAGNETIC CALCULATIONS.

For the Use of Electrical Engineers and Artisans, Teachers, Students, and all others interested in the Theory and Application of Electricity and Magnetism. By A. A. ATKINSON, Professor of Electricity in Ohio University. Crown 8vo, cloth . . . . *Net* **9/0**
" To teachers and those who already possess a fair knowledge of their subject we can recommend this book as being useful to consult when requiring data or formulæ which it is neither convenient nor necessary to retain by memory."—*The Electrician.*

SUBMARINE TELEGRAPHS.

Their History, Construction. and Working. Founded in part on WÜNSCHENDORFF's " Traité de Télégraphie Sous-Marine," and Compiled from Authoritative and Exclusive Sources. By CHARLES BRIGHT, F.R.S.E., A.M.Inst.C.E., M.I E.E. 780 pp., fully Illustrated, including Maps and Folding Plates. Royal 8vo, cloth . . . . *Net* **£3 3s.**
" There are few, if any, persons more fitted to write a treatise on submarine telegraphy than Mr. Charles Bright. He has done his work admirably, and has written in a way which will appeal as much to the layman as to the engineer. This admirable volume must, for many years to come, hold the position of the English classic on submarine telegraphy."—*Engineer.*
" This book is full of information. It makes a book of reference which should be in every engineer's library."—*Nature.*
" Mr. Bright's interestingly written and admirably illustrated book will meet with a welcome reception from cable men."—*Electrician.*
" The author deals with his subject from all points of view—political and strategical as well as scientific. The work will be of interest, not only to men of science, but to the general public. We can strongly recommend it."—*Athenæum.*

THE ELECTRICAL ENGINEER'S POCKET-BOOK.

Consisting of Modern Rules, Formulæ, Tables, and Data. By H. R. KEMPE, M.I.E.E., A.M.Inst.C.E., Technical Officer Postal Telegraphs, Author of " A Handbook of Electrical Testing," &c. Second Edition, thoroughly Revised, with Additions. With numerous Illustrations. Royal 32mo, oblong, leather **5/0**
" It is the best book of its kind."—*Electrical Engineer.*
" The Electrical Engineer's Pocket-Book is a good one."—*Electrician.*
" Strongly recommended to those engaged in the electrical industries."—*Electrical Review.*

POWER TRANSMITTED BY ELECTRICITY.

And applied by the Electric Motor, including Electric Railway Construction. By P. ATKINSON, A.M., Ph.D. Third Edition, Fully Revised, and New Matter added. With 94 Illustrations. Crown 8vo, cloth . . *Net* **9/0**

DYNAMIC ELECTRICITY AND MAGNETISM.

By PHILIP ATKINSON, A.M., Ph.D., Author of " Elements of Static Electricity," &c. Crown 8vo, 417 pp., with 120 Illustrations, cloth . **10/6**

THE MANAGEMENT OF DYNAMOS.

A Handybook of Theory and Practice for the Use of Mechanics, Engineers, Students, and others in Charge of Dynamos. By G. W. LUMMIS-PATERSON. Third Edition, Revised. Crown 8vo, cloth **4/6**
" An example which deserves to be taken as a model by other authors. The subject is treated in a manner which any intelligent man who is fit to be entrusted with charge of an engine should be able to understand. It is a useful book to all who make, tend, or employ electric machinery."
—Architect.

THE STANDARD ELECTRICAL DICTIONARY.

A Popular Encyclopædia of Words and Terms Used in the Practice of Electrical Engineering. Containing upwards of 3,000 definitions, By T. O'CONOR SLOANE, A.M., Ph.D. Third Edition, with Appendix. Crown 8vo, 690 pp., 390 Illustrations, cloth . . . . *Net* **7/6**
" The work has many attractive features in it, and is, beyond doubt, a well put together and useful publication. The amount of ground covered may be gathered from the fact that in the index about 5,000 references will be found."*—Electrical Review.*

ELECTRIC LIGHT FITTING.

A Handbook for Working Electrical Engineers, embodying Practical Notes on Installation Management. By J. W. URQUHART, Electrician, Author of " Electric Light," &c. With numerous Illustrations. Third Edition, Revised, with Additions. Crown 8vo, cloth **5/0**
" This volume deals with the mechanics of electric lighting, and is addressed to men who are already engaged in the work, or are training for it. The work traverses a great deal of ground, and may be read as a sequel to the author's useful work on ' Electric Light.'"*—Electrician.*
" The book is well worth the perusal of the workman, for whom it is written."*—Electrical Review.*

ELECTRIC LIGHT.

Its Production and Use, Embodying Plain Directions for the Treatment of Dynamo-Electric Machines, Batteries, Accumulators, and Electric Lamps. By J. W. URQUHART, C.E. Sixth Edition, Enlarged. Crown 8vo, cloth.
7/6
" The whole ground of electric lighting is more or less covered and explained in a very clear and concise manner."*—Electrical Review.*
" A *vade-mecum* of the salient facts connected with the science of electric lighting."*— Electrician.*

DYNAMO CONSTRUCTION.

A Practical Handbook for the Use of Engineer-Constructors and Electricians-in-Charge. Embracing Framework Building, Field Magnet and Armature Winding and Grouping, Compounding, &c. By J. W. URQUHART. Second Edition, Enlarged, with 114 Illustrations. Crown 8vo, cloth . . **7/6**
" Mr. Urquhart's book is the first one which deals with these matters in such a way that the engineering student can understand them. The book is very readable, and the author leads his rea·lers up to difficult subjects by reasonably simple tests."*—Engineering Review*

ELECTRIC SHIP-LIGHTING.

A Handbook on the Practical Fitting and Running of Ships' Electrical Plant. For the Use of Shipowners and Builders, Marine Electricians, and Seagoing Engineers-in-Charge. By J. W. URQUHART, C.E. Second Edition, Revised and Extended. With 88 Illustrations, Crown 8vo, cloth **7/6**
" The subject of ship electric lighting is one of vast importance and Mr. Urquhart is to be highly complimented for placing such a valuable work at the service of marine electricians."*—The Steamship.*

ELECTRIC LIGHTING (ELEMENTARY PRINCIPLES OF).

By ALAN A. CAMPBELL SWINTON, M.Inst.C.E., M.I.E.E. Fifth Edition. With 16 Illustrations. Crown 8vo, cloth **1/6**

ELECTRIC LIGHT FOR COUNTRY HOUSES.

A Practical Handbook on the Erection and Running of Small Installations, with Particulars of the Cost of Plant and Working. By J. H. KNIGHT. Third Edition, Revised. Crown 8vo, wrapper **1/0**

HOW TO MAKE A DYNAMO.

A Practical Treatise for Amateurs. Containing Illustrations and Detailed Instructions for Constructing a Small Dynamo to Produce the Electric Light. By ALFRED CROFTS. Sixth Edition, Revised. Crown 8vo, cloth . **2/0**

THE STUDENT'S TEXT-BOOK OF ELECTRICITY.

By H. M. NOAD, F.R.S. 650 pp., with 470 Illustrations. Crown 8vo, cloth.
9/0

ARCHITECTURE, BUILDING, ETC.

PRACTICAL BUILDING CONSTRUCTION.

A Handbook for Students Preparing for Examinations, and a Book of Reference for Persons Engaged in Building. By JOHN PARNELL ALLEN, Surveyor, Lecturer on Building Construction at the Durham College of Science, Newcastle-on-Tyne. Fourth Edition, Revised and Enlarged. Medium 8vo, 570 pp., with 1,000 Illustrations, cloth.

[Just Published. Net **7/6**

" The most complete exposition of building construction we have seen. It contains all that is necessary to prepare students for the various examinations in building construction."—*Building News.*

" The author depends nearly as much on his diagrams as on his type. The pages suggest the hand of a man of experience in building operations—and the volume must be a blessing to many teachers as well as to students."—*The Architect.*

" The work is sure to prove a formidable rival to great and small competitors alike, and bids fair to take a permanent place as a favourite student's text-book. The large number of illustrations deserve particular mention for the great merit they possess for purposes of reference in exactly corresponding to convenient scales."—*Journal of the Royal Institute of British Architects.*

PRACTICAL MASONRY.

A Guide to the Art of Stone Cutting. Comprising the Construction, Setting Out, and Working of Stairs, Circular Work, Arches, Niches, Domes, Pendentives, Vaults, Tracery Windows, &c. ; to which are added Supplements relating to Masonry Estimating and Quantity Surveying, and to Building Stones, and a Glossary of Terms. For the Use of Students, Masons, and other Workmen. By WILLIAM R. PURCHASE, Building Inspector to the Borough of Hove. Fourth Edition, Enlarged. Royal 8vo, 210 pp., with 52 Lithographic Plates, comprising over 400 Diagrams, cloth.

[Just Published. Net **7/6**

" Mr. Purchase's 'Practical Masonry' will undoubtedly be found useful to all interested in this important subject, whether theoretically or practically. Most of the examples given are from actual work carried out, the diagrams being carefully drawn. The book is a practical treatise on the subject, the author himself having commenced as an operative mason, and afterwards acted as foreman mason on many large and important buildings prior to the attainment of his present position. It should be found of general utility to architectural students and others, as well as to those to whom it is specially addressed."—*Journal of the Royal Institute of British Architects.*

MODERN PLUMBING, STEAM AND HOT WATER HEATING.

A New Practical Work for the Plumber, the Heating Engineer, the Architect, and the Builder. By J. J. LAWLER, Author of "American Sanitary Plumbing," &c. With 284 Illustrations and Folding Plates. 4to, cloth . *Net* **21/-**

HEATING BY HOT WATER,

VENTILATION AND HOT WATER SUPPLY.

By WALTER JONES, M.I.M.E. 340 pages, with 140 Illustrations. Royal 8vo, cloth. *[Just Published. Net* **6.0**

CONCRETE : ITS NATURE AND USES.

A Book for Architects, Builders, Contractors, and Clerks of Works. By GEORGE L. SUTCLIFFE, A.R.I.B.A. 350 pp., with Illustrations. Crown 8vo, cloth **7/6**

" The author treats a difficult subject in a lucid manner. The manual fills a long-felt gap. It is careful and exhaustive ; equally useful as a student's guide and an architect's book of reference."—*Journal of the Royal Institute of British Architects.*

LOCKWOOD'S BUILDER'S PRICE BOOK for 1904.

A Comprehensive Handbook of the Latest Prices and Data for Builders, Architects, Engineers, and Contractors. Re-constructed, Re-written, and Greatly Enlarged. By FRANCIS T. W. MILLER. 800 closely-printed pages, crown 8vo, cloth **4/0**

" This book is a very useful one, and should find a place in every English office connected with the building and engineering professions."—*Industries.*

" An excellent book of reference."—*Architect.*

" In its new and revised form this Price Book is what a work of this kind should be—comprehensive, reliable, well arranged, legible, and well bound."—*British Architect.*

DECORATIVE PART OF CIVIL ARCHITECTURE.

By Sir WILLIAM CHAMBERS, F.R.S. With Portrait, Illustrations, Notes, and an EXAMINATION OF GRECIAN ARCHITECTURE, by JOSEPH GWILT, F.S.A. Revised and Edited by W. H. LEEDS. 66 Plates, 4to, cloth . . **21/0**

THE MECHANICS OF ARCHITECTURE.

A Treatise on Applied Mechanics, especially Adapted to the Use of Architects. By E. W. TARN, M.A., Author of " The Science of Building," &c. Second Edition, Enlarged. Illustrated with 125 Diagrams. Crown 8vo, cloth **7/6**

" The book is a very useful and helpful manual of architectural mechanics."—*Builder.*

A HANDY BOOK OF VILLA ARCHITECTURE.

Being a Series of Designs for Villa Residences in various Styles. With Outline Specifications and Estimates. By C. WICKES, Architect, Author of " The Spires and Towers of England," &c. 61 Plates, 4to, half-morocco, gilt edges . . . . **£1 11s. 6o.**

" The whole of the designs bear evidence of their being the work of an artistic architect, and they will prove very valuable and suggestive."—*Building News.*

THE ARCHITECT'S GUIDE.

Being a Text-book of Useful Information for Architects, Engineers, Surveyors, Contractors, Clerks of Works, &c., &c. By F. ROGERS. Crown 8vo, cloth. **3/6**

ARCHITECTURAL PERSPECTIVE.

The whole Course and Operations of the Draughtsman in Drawing a Large House in Linear Perspective. Illustrated by 43 Folding Plates. By F. O. FERGUSON. Third Edition. 8vo, boards **3/6**

" It is the most intelligible of the treatises on this ill-treated subject that I have met with."— E. INGRESS BELL, ESQ., in the *R.I.B.A. Journal.*

PRACTICAL RULES ON DRAWING.

For the Operative Builder and Young Student in Architecture. By GEORGE PYNE. 14 Plates, 4to, boards **7/6**

MEASURING AND VALUING ARTIFICERS' WORK

(The Student's Guide to the Practice of). Containing Directions for taking Dimensions, Abstracting the same, and bringing the Quantities into Bill, with Tables of Constants for Valuation of Labour, and for the Calculation of Areas and Solidities. Originally edited by E. DOBSON, Architect. With Additions by E. W. TARN, M.A. Seventh Edition, Revised. With 8 Plates and 63 Woodcuts. Crown 8vo, cloth. **7/6**

" This edition will be found the most complete treatise on the principles of measuring and valuing artificers' work that has yet been published."—*Building News.*

TECHNICAL GUIDE, MEASURER, AND ESTIMATOR.

For Builders and Surveyors. Containing Technical Directions for Measuring Work in all the Building Trades, Complete Specifications for Houses, Roads, and Drains, and an Easy Method of Estimating the parts of a Building collectively. By A. C. BEATON. Ninth Edition. Waistcoat-pocket size, gilt edges **1/6**

" No builder, architect, surveyor, or valuer should be without his ' Beaton.'"—*Building News.*

SPECIFICATIONS FOR PRACTICAL ARCHITECTURE.

A Guide to the Architect, Engineer, Surveyor, and Builder. With an Essay on the Structure and Science of Modern Buildings. Upon the Basis of the Work by ALFRED BARTHOLOMEW, thoroughly Revised, Corrected, and greatly added to by FREDERICK ROGERS, Architect. Third Edition, Revised. 8vo, cloth **15/0**

" The work is too well known to need any recommendation from us. It is one of the books with which every young architect must be equipped."—*Architect.*

THE HOUSE-OWNER'S ESTIMATOR.

Or, What will it Cost to Build, Alter, or Repair? A Price Book for Un-professional People as well as the Architectural Surveyor and Builder. By J. D. SIMON. Edited by F. T. W. MILLER, A.R.I.B.A. Fifth Edition. Carefully Revised. Crown 8vo, cloth. . . . . . . *Net* **3/6**

" In two years it will repay its cost a hundred times over."—*Field.*

SANITATION AND WATER SUPPLY.

THE HEALTH OFFICER'S POCKET-BOOK.

A Guide to Sanitary Practice and Law. For Medical Officers of Health, Sanitary Inspectors, Members of Sanitary Authorities, &c. By EDWARD F. WILLOUGHBY, M.D. (Lond.), &c. Second Edition, Revised and Enlarged. Fcap. 8vo, leather . . . . *Net* **10/6**

" It is a mine of condensed information of a pertinent and useful kind on the various subjects of which it treats. The different subjects are succinctly but fully and scientifically dealt with."— *The Lancet.*

" We recommend all those engaged in practical sanitary work to furnish themselves with a copy for reference."—*Sanitary Journal.*

THE BACTERIAL PURIFICATION OF SEWAGE:

Being a Practical Account of the Various Modern Biological Methods of Purifying Sewage. By SIDNEY BARWISE, M.D. (Lond.), D.P.H. (Camb.), etc. With 10 Page Plates and 2 Folding Diagrams. Royal 8vo, cloth.
Net **6/0**

THE PURIFICATION OF SEWAGE.

Being a Brief Account of the Scientific Principles of Sewage Purification, and their Practical Application. By SIDNEY BARWISE, M.D. (Lond.), M.R.C.S., D.P.H. (Camb.), Fellow of the Sanitary Institute, Medical Officer of Health to the Derbyshire County Council. Crown 8vo, cloth **5/0**

WATER AND ITS PURIFICATION.

A Handbook for the Use of Local Authorities, Sanitary Officers, and others interested in Water Supply. By S. RIDEAL, D.Sc. Lond., F.I.C. Second Edition, Revised, with Additions, including numerous Illustrations and Tables. Large Crown 8vo, cloth . . . . *Net* **9/0**

RURAL WATER SUPPLY.

A Practical Handbook on the Supply of Water and Construction of Water-works for Small Country Districts. By ALLAN GREENWELL, A.M.I.C.E., and W. T. CURRY, A.M.I.C.E. Revised Edition. Crown 8vo, cloth **5/0**

THE WATER SUPPLY OF CITIES AND TOWNS.

By WILLIAM HUMBER, A.M. Inst. C.E., and M.Inst. M.E. Imp. 4to, half-bound morocco. (See page 11.) . . . . . . *Net* **£6 6s.**

THE WATER SUPPLY OF TOWNS AND THE CON-STRUCTION OF WATER-WORKS.

By PROFESSOR W. K. BURTON, A.M. Inst. C.E. Second Edition, Revised and Extended. Royal 8vo, cloth. (See page 10.) . . . . **£1 5s.**

WATER ENGINEERING.

A Practical Treatise on the Measurement, Storage, Conveyance, and Utilisation of Water for the Supply of Towns. By C. SLAGG, A.M. Inst. C.E. **7/6**

SANITARY WORK IN SMALL TOWNS AND VILLAGES.

By CHARLES SLAGG, A. M. Inst. C.E. Crown 8vo, cloth . . . **3/0**

PLUMBING.

A Text-book to the Practice of the Art or Craft of the Plumber. By W. P. BUCHAN. Ninth Edition, Enlarged, with 500 Illustrations. Crown 8vo, **3/6**

VENTILATION.

A Text-book to the Practice of the Art of Ventilating Buildings. By W. P. BUCHAN, R.P. Crown 8vo, cloth **3/6**

CARPENTRY, TIMBER, ETC.

THE ELEMENTARY PRINCIPLES OF CARPENTRY.

A Treatise on the Pressure and Equilibrium of Timber Framing, the Resistance of Timber, and the Construction of Floors, Arches, Bridges, Roofs, Uniting Iron and Stone with Timber, &c. To which is added an Essay on the Nature and Properties of Timber, &c., with Descriptions of the kinds of Wood used in Building; also numerous Tables of the Scantlings of Timber for different purposes, the Specific Gravities of Materials, &c. By THOMAS TREDGOLD, C.E. With an Appendix of Specimens of Various Roofs of Iron and Stone, Illustrated. Seventh Edition, thoroughly Revised and considerably Enlarged by E. WYNDHAM TARN, M.A., Author of "The Science of Building," &c. With 61 Plates, Portrait of the Author, and several Woodcuts. In One large Vol., 4to, cloth . . . . £1 5s.

"Ought to be in every architect's and every builder's library."—*Builder.*
"A work whose monumental excellence must commend it wherever skilful carpentry is concerned. The author's principles are rather confirmed than impaired by time. The additional plates are of great intrinsic value."—*Building News.*

WOODWORKING MACHINERY.

Its Rise, Progress, and Construction. With Hints on the Management of Saw Mills and the Economical Conversion of Timber. Illustrated with Examples of Recent Designs by leading English, French, and American Engineers. By M. POWIS BALE, A.M.Inst.C.E., M.I.M.E. Second Edition, Revised, with large Additions, large crown 8vo, 440 pp., cloth 9/0

"Mr. Bale is evidently an expert on the subject, and he has collected so much information that his book is all-sufficient for builders and others engaged in the conversion of timber."—*Architect.*
"The most comprehensive compendium of wood-working machinery we have seen. The author is a thorough master of his subject."—*Building News.*

SAW MILLS.

Their Arrangement and Management, and the Economical Conversion of Timber. By M. POWIS BALE, A.M.Inst.C.E. Second Edition, Revised. Crown 8vo, cloth. 10/6

"The *administration* of a large sawing establishment is discussed, and the subject examined from a financial standpoint. Hence the size, shape, order, and disposition of saw mills and the like are gone into in detail, and the course of the timber is traced from its reception to its delivery in its converted state. We could not desire a more complete or practical treatise."—*Builder.*

THE CARPENTER'S GUIDE.

Or, Book of Lines for Carpenters; comprising all the Elementary Principles essential for acquiring a knowledge of Carpentry. Founded on the late PETER NICHOLSON's standard work. A New Edition, Revised by ARTHUR ASHPITEL, F.S.A. Together with Practical Rules on Drawing, by GEORGE PYNE. With 74 Plates, 4to, cloth . . . . £1 1s.

A PRACTICAL TREATISE ON HANDRAILING.

Showing New and Simple Methods for Finding the Pitch of the Plank, Drawing the Moulds, Bevelling, Jointing-up, and Squaring the Wreath. By GEORGE COLLINGS. Revised and Enlarged, to which is added A TREATISE ON STAIR-BUILDING. Third Edition. With Plates and Diagrams. 12mo, cloth. 2/6

"Will be found of practical utility in the execution of this difficult branch of joinery."—*Builder.*
"Almost every difficult phase of this somewhat intricate branch of joinery is elucidated by the aid of plates and explanatory letterpress."—*Furniture Gazette.*

CIRCULAR WORK IN CARPENTRY AND JOINERY.

A Practical Treatise on Circular Work of Single and Double Curvature. By GEORGE COLLINGS. With Diagrams. Fourth Edition, 12mo, cloth . 2/6

"An excellent example of what a book of this kind should be. Cheap in price, clear in definition, and practical in the examples selected."—*Builder.*

THE CABINET-MAKER'S GUIDE TO THE ENTIRE CONSTRUCTION OF CABINET WORK.

By RICHARD BITMEAD. Illustrated with Plans, Sections and Working Drawings. Crown 8vo, cloth 2/6

HANDRAILING COMPLETE IN EIGHT LESSONS.

On the Square-Cut System. By J. S. GOLDTHORP, Teacher of Geometry and Building Construction at the Halifax Mechanics' Institute.   With Eight Plates and over 150 Practical Exercises.   4to, cloth **3/6**

"Likely to be of considerable value to joiners and others who take a pride in good work. The arrangement of the book is excellent.   We heartily commend it to teachers and students."— *Timber Trades Journal.*

TIMBER MERCHANT'S and BUILDER'S COMPANION.

Containing New and Copious Tables of the Reduced Weight and Measurement of Deals and Battens, of all sizes, and other Useful Tables for the use of Timber Merchants and Builders.   By WILLIAM DOWSING.   Fourth Edition, Revised and Corrected.   Crown 8vo, cloth **3/0**

"We are glad to see a fourth edition of these admirable tables, which for correctness and simplicity of arrangement leave nothing to be desired."—*Timber Trades Journal.*

THE PRACTICAL TIMBER MERCHANT.

Being a Guide for the Use of Building Contractors, Surveyors, Builders, &c., comprising useful Tables for all purposes connected with the Timber Trade, Marks of Wood, Essay on the Strength of Timber, Remarks on the Growth of Timber, &c.   By W. RICHARDSON.   Second Edition.   Fcap. 8vo, cloth . **3/6**

"This handy manual contains much valuable information for the use of timber merchants, builders, foresters, and all others connected with the growth, sale, and manufacture of timber."— *Journal of Forestry.*

PACKING-CASE TABLES.

Showing the number of Superficial Feet in Boxes or Packing-Cases, from six inches square and upwards.   By W. RICHARDSON, Timber Broker.   Third Edition.   Oblong 4to, cloth **3/6**

"Invaluable labour-saving tables."—*Ironmonger.*
"Will save much labour and calculation."—*Grocer.*

GUIDE TO SUPERFICIAL MEASUREMENT.

Tables calculated from 1 to 200 inches in length by 1 to 108 inches in breadth. For the use of Architects, Surveyors, Engineers, Timber Merchants, Builders, &c.   By JAMES HAWKINGS.   Fifth Edition.   Fcap., cloth. **3/6**

"These tables will be found of great assistance to all who require to make calculations of superficial measurement."—*English Mechanic.*

PRACTICAL FORESTRY.

And its Bearing on the Improvement of Estates.   By CHARLES E. CURTIS, F.S.I., Professor of Forestry, Field Engineering, and General Estate Management, at the College of Agriculture, Downton.   Second Edition, Revised.   Crown 8vo, cloth **3/6**

PREFATORY REMARKS. — OBJECTS OF PLANTING. — CHOICE OF A FORESTER. — CHOICE OF SOIL AND SITE.—LAYING OUT OF LAND FOR PLANTATIONS.—PREPARATION OF THE GROUND FOR PLANTING. —DRAINAGE.—PLANTING.—DISTANCES AND DISTRIBUTION OF TREES IN PLANTATIONS.—TREES AND GROUND GAME.—ATTENTION AFTER PLANTING.—THINNING OF PLANTATIONS. — PRUNING OF FOREST TREES.—REALIZATION. —METHODS OF SALE.—MEASUREMENT OF TIMBER.—MEASUREMENT AND VALUATION OF LARCH PLANTATION.—FIRE LINES.—COST OF PLANTING.

"Mr. Curtis has in the course of a series of short pithy chapters afforded much information of a useful and practical character on the planting and subsequent treatment of trees."— *Illustrated Carpenter and Builder.*

THE ELEMENTS OF FORESTRY.

Designed to afford Information concerning the Planting and Care of Forest Trees for Ornament or Profit, with suggestions upon the Creation and Care of Woodlands.   By F. B. HOUGH.   Large crown 8vo, cloth   .   .   . **10/0**

TIMBER IMPORTER'S, TIMBER MERCHANT'S, AND BUILDER'S STANDARD GUIDE.

By RICHARD E. GRANDY.   Comprising:—An Analysis of Deal Standards, Home and Foreign, with Comparative Values and Tabular Arrangements for fixing Net Landed Cost on Baltic and North American Deals, including all intermediate Expenses, Freight, Insurance, &c.; together with copious Information for the Retailer and Builder.   Third Edition, Revised.   12mo, cloth **2/0**

"Everything it pretends to be: built up gradually, it leads one from a forest to a treenail, and throws in, as a makeweight, a host of material concerning bricks, columns, cisterns, &c."—*English Mechanic.*

DECORATIVE ARTS, ETC.

SCHOOL OF PAINTING FOR THE IMITATION OF WOODS AND MARBLES.

As Taught and Practised by A. R. VAN DER BURG and P. VAN DER BURG, Directors of the Rotterdam Painting Institution. Royal folio, 18½ by 12½ in., Illustrated with 24 full-size Coloured Plates; also 12 plain Plates, comprising 154 Figures. Fourth Edition cloth . *[Just Published.* Net **£1 5s.**

LIST OF PLATES.

1. VARIOUS TOOLS REQUIRED FOR WOOD PAINTING.—2, 3. WALNUT; PRELIMINARY STAGES OF GRAINING AND FINISHED SPECIMEN. — 4. TOOLS USED FOR MARBLE PAINTING AND METHOD OF MANIPULATION.—5, 6. ST. REMI MARBLE; EARLIER OPERATIONS AND FINISHED SPECIMEN. — 7. METHODS OF SKETCHING DIFFERENT GRAINS, KNOTS, &c.—8, 9. ASH: PRELIMINARY STAGES AND FINISHED SPECIMEN. — 10. METHODS OF SKETCHING MARBLE GRAINS. — 11, 12. BRECHE MARBLE; PRELIMINARY STAGES OF WORKING AND FINISHED SPECIMEN.—13. MAPLE; METHODS OF PRODUCING THE DIFFERENT GRAINS.—14, 15. BIRD'S-EYE MAPLE; PRELIMINARY STAGES AND FINISHED SPECIMEN.—16. METHODS OF SKETCHING THE DIFFERENT SPECIES OF WHITE MARBLE.—17, 18. WHITE MARBLE; PRELIMINARY STAGES OF PROCESS AND FINISHED SPECIMEN.—19. MAHOGANY; SPECIMENS OF VARIOUS GRAINS AND METHODS OF MANIPULATION.—20, 21. MAHOGANY; EARLIER STAGES AND FINISHED SPECIMEN.—22, 23, 24. SIENNA MARBLE; VARIETIES OF GRAIN, PRELIMINARY STAGES AND FINISHED SPECIMEN.—25, 26, 27. JUNIPER WOOD; METHODS OF PRODUCING GRAIN, &c.; PRELIMINARY STAGES AND FINISHED SPECIMEN.—28, 29, 30. VERT DE MER MARBLE; VARIETIES OF GRAIN AND METHODS OF WORKING, UNFINISHED AND FINISHED SPECIMENS.—31, 32, 33. OAK; VARIETIES OF GRAIN, TOOLS EMPLOYED AND METHODS OF MANIPULATION, PRELIMINARY STAGES AND FINISHED SPECIMEN.—34, 35, 36. WAULSORT MARBLE; VARIETIES OF GRAIN, UNFINISHED AND FINISHED SPECIMENS.

"Those who desire to attain skill in the art of painting woods and marbles will find advantage in consulting this book. . . . Some of the Working Men's Clubs should give their young men the opportunity to study it."—*Builder.*

"A comprehensive guide to the art. The explanations of the processes, the manipulation and management of the colours, and the beautifully executed plates will not be the least valuable to the student who aims at making his work a faithful transcript of nature."—*Building News.*

"Students and novices are fortunate who are able to become the possessors of so noble a work."—*The Architect.*

ELEMENTARY DECORATION.

A Guide to the Simpler Forms of Everyday Art. Together with PRACTICAL HOUSE DECORATION. By JAMES W. FACEY. With numerous Illustrations. In One Vol., strongly half-bound **5/0**

HOUSE PAINTING, GRAINING, MARBLING, AND SIGN WRITING.

A Practical Manual of. By ELLIS A. DAVIDSON. Eighth Edition. With Coloured Plates and Wood Engravings. Crown 8vo, cloth . . . **6/0**

"A mass of information of use to the amateur and of value to the practical man."—*English Mechanic.*

THE DECORATOR'S ASSISTANT.

A Modern Guide for Decorative Artists and Amateurs, Painters, Writers, Gilders, &c. Containing upwards of 600 Receipts, Rules, and Instructions; with a variety of Information for General Work connected with every Class of Interior and Exterior Decorations, &c. Eighth Edition. Cr. 8vo . **1/0**

"Full of receipts of value to decorators, painters, gilders, &c. The book contains the gist of larger treatises on colour and technical processes. It would be difficult to meet with a work so full of varied information on the painter's art."—*Building News.*

MARBLE DECORATION

And the Terminology of British and Foreign Marbles. A Handbook for Students. By GEORGE H. BLAGROVE, Author of "Shoring and its Application," &c. With 28 Illustrations. Crown 8vo, cloth . . . **3/6**

"This most useful and much wanted handbook should be in the hands of every architect and builder."—*Building World.*

"A carefully and usefully written treatise; the work is essentially practical."—*Scotsman.*

DELAMOTTE'S WORKS ON ILLUMINATION AND ALPHABETS.

ORNAMENTAL ALPHABETS, ANCIENT & MEDIÆVAL.

From the Eighth Century, with Numerals; including Gothic, Church-Text, large and small, German, Italian, Arabesque, Initials for Illumination, Monograms, Crosses, &c., &c., for the use of Architectural and Engineering Draughtsmen, Missal Painters, Masons, Decorative Painters, Lithographers, Engravers, Carvers, &c. Collected and Engraved by F. DELAMOTTE, and printed in Colours. New and Cheaper Edition. Royal 8vo, oblong, ornamental boards **2/6**

" For those who insert enamelled sentences round gilded chalices, who blazon shop legends over shop-doors, who letter church walls with pithy sentences from the Decalogue, this book will be useful."—*Athenæum.*

MODERN ALPHABETS, PLAIN AND ORNAMENTAL.

Including German, Old English, Saxon, Italic, Perspective, Greek, Hebrew, Court Hand, Engrossing, Tuscan, Riband, Gothic, Rustic, and Arabesque ; with several Original Designs, and an Analysis of the Roman and Old English Alphabets, large and small, and Numerals, for the use of Draughtsmen, Surveyors, Masons, Decorative Painters, Lithographers, Engravers, Carvers, &c. Collected and Engraved by F. DELAMOTTE, and printed in Colours. New and Cheaper Edition. Royal 8vo, oblong, ornamental boards . **2/6**

" There is comprised in it every possible shape into which the letters of the alphabet and numerals can be formed, and the talent which has been expended in the conception of the various plain and ornamental letters is wonderful."—*Standard.*

MEDIÆVAL ALPHABETS AND INITIALS.

By F. G. DELAMOTTE. Containing 21 Plates and Illuminated Title, printed in Gold and Colours. With an Introduction by J. WILLIS BROOKS. Fifth Edition. Small 4to, ornamental boards . . . . . . *Net* **5/0**

"A volume in which the letters of the alphabet come forth glorified in gilding and all the colours of the prism interwoven and intertwined and intermingled."—*Sun.*

A PRIMER OF THE ART OF ILLUMINATION.

For the Use of Beginners ; with a Rudimentary Treatise on the Art, Practical Directions for its Exercise, and Examples taken from Illuminated MSS., printed in Gold and Colours. By F. DELAMOTTE. New and Cheaper Edition. Small 4to, ornamental boards **6/0**

" The examples of ancient MSS. recommended to the student, which, with much good sense, the author chooses from collections accessible to all, are selected with judgment and knowledge as well as taste."—*Athenæum.*

THE EMBROIDERER'S BOOK OF DESIGN.

Containing Initials, Emblems, Cyphers, Monograms, Ornamental Borders, Ecclesiastical Devices, Mediæval and Modern Alphabets, and National Emblems. Collected by F. DELAMOTTE, and printed in Colours. Oblong royal 8vo, ornamental wrapper . . . . *Net* **2/0**

" The book will be of great assistance to ladies and young children who are endowed with the art of plying the needle in this most ornamental and useful pretty work."—*East Anglian Times.*

WOOD-CARVING FOR AMATEURS.

With Hints on Design. By A LADY. With 10 Plates. New and Cheaper Edition. Crown 8vo, in emblematic wrapper **2/0**

" The handicraft of the wood-carver, so well as a book can impart it, may be learnt from ' A Lady's ' publication."—*Athenæum.*

PAINTING POPULARLY EXPLAINED.

By THOMAS JOHN GULLICK, Painter, and JOHN TIMBS, F.S.A. Including Fresco, Oil, Mosaic, Water-Colour, Water-Glass, Tempera, Encaustic, Miniature, Painting on Ivory, Vellum, Pottery, Enamel, Glass, &c. Fifth Edition. Crown 8vo, cloth **5/0**

⁎ *Adopted as a Prize Book at South Kensington.*

" Much may be learned, even by those who fancy they do not require to be taught, from the careful perusal of this unpretending but comprehensive treatise."—*Art Journal.*

NATURAL SCIENCE, ETC.

THE VISIBLE UNIVERSE.
Chapters on the Origin and Construction of the Heavens. By J. E. GORE, F.R.A.S., Author of "Star Groups," &c. Illustrated by 6 Stellar Photographs and 12 Plates. Demy 8vo, cloth **16/0**

STAR GROUPS.
A Student's Guide to the Constellations. By J. ELLARD GORE, F.R.A.S., M.R.I.A., &c., Author of "The Visible Universe," "The Scenery of the Heavens," &c. With 30 Maps. Small 4to, cloth **5/0**

AN ASTRONOMICAL GLOSSARY.
Or, Dictionary of Terms used in Astronomy. With Tables of Data and Lists of Remarkable and Interesting Celestial Objects. By J. ELLARD GORE, F.R.A.S., Author of "The Visible Universe," &c. Small crown 8vo, cloth. **2/6**

THE MICROSCOPE.
Its Construction and Management. Including Technique, Photo-micrography, and the Past and Future of the Microscope. By Dr. HENRI VAN HEURCK. Re-Edited and Augmented from the Fourth French Edition, and Translated by WYNNE E. BAXTER, F.G.S. Imp. 8vo, cloth **18/0**

A MANUAL OF THE MOLLUSCA.
A Treatise on Recent and Fossil Shells. By S. P. WOODWARD, A.L.S., F.G.S. With an Appendix on RECENT AND FOSSIL CONCHOLOGICAL DISCOVERIES, by RALPH TATE, A.L.S., F.G.S. With 23 Plates and upwards of 300 Woodcuts. Reprint of Fourth Edition (1880). Crown 8vo, cloth. **7/6**

THE TWIN RECORDS OF CREATION.
Or, Geology and Genesis, their Perfect Harmony and Wonderful Concord. By G. W. V. LE VAUX. 8vo, cloth **5/0**

LARDNER'S HANDBOOKS OF SCIENCE.
HANDBOOK OF MECHANICS.
Enlarged and re-written by B. LOEWY, F.R.A.S. Post 8vo, cloth . **6/0**
HANDBOOK OF HYDROSTATICS AND PNEUMATICS.
Revised and Enlarged by B. LOEWY, F.R.A.S. Post 8vo, cloth . **5/0**
HANDBOOK OF HEAT.
Edited and re-written by B. LOEWY, F.R.A.S. Post 8vo, cloth . **6/0**
HANDBOOK OF OPTICS.
New Edition. Edited by T. OLVER HARDING, B.A. Small 8vo, cloth **5/0**
ELECTRICITY, MAGNETISM, AND ACOUSTICS.
Edited by GEO. C. FOSTER, B.A. Small 8vo, cloth **5/0**
HANDBOOK OF ASTRONOMY.
Revised and Edited by EDWIN DUNKIN, F.R.A.S. 8vo, cloth . . **9/6**
MUSEUM OF SCIENCE AND ART.
With upwards of 1,200 Engravings. In Six Double Volumes, £1 1s. Cloth, or half-morocco . . . . £1 11s. 6D.
NATURAL PHILOSOPHY FOR SCHOOLS . . **3/6**
ANIMAL PHYSIOLOGY FOR SCHOOLS . . **3,6**
THE ELECTRIC TELEGRAPH.
Revised by E. B. BRIGHT, F.R.A.S. Fcap. 8vo, cloth . **2/6**

L.   c

CHEMICAL MANUFACTURES,
CHEMISTRY, ETC.

THE OIL FIELDS OF RUSSIA AND THE RUSSIAN PETROLEUM INDUSTRY.

A Practical Handbook on the Exploration, Exploitation, and Management of Russian Oil Properties, including Notes on the Origin of Petroleum in Russia, a Description of the Theory and Practice of Liquid Fuel, and a Translation of the Rules and Regulations concerning Russian Oil Properties. By A. BEEBY THOMPSON, A.M.I.M.E., late Chief Engineer and Manager of the European Petroleum Company's Russian Oil Properties. About 500 pp., with numerous Illustrations and Photographic Plates, and a Map of the Balakhany-Saboontchy-Romany Oil Field. Super-royal 8vo, cloth.

[*Just Published. Net* **£3 3s.**

THE ANALYSIS OF OILS AND ALLIED SUBSTANCES.

By A. C. WRIGHT, M.A.Oxon., B.Sc.Lond, formerly Assistant Lecturer in Chemistry at the Yorkshire College, Leeds, and Lecturer in Chemistry at the Hull Technical School. Demy 8vo, cloth. . . . . . *Net* **9/0**

THE GAS ENGINEER'S POCKET-BOOK.

Comprising Tables, Notes and Memoranda relating to the Manufacture, Distribution and Use of Coal Gas and the Construction of Gas Works. By H. O'CONNOR, A.M.Inst.C.E. Second Edition, Revised. 470 pp., crown 8vo, fully Illustrated, leather **10/6**

"The book contains a vast amount of information. The author goes consecutively through the engineering details and practical methods involved in each of the different processes or parts of a gas-works. He has certainly succeeded in making a compilation of hard matters of fact absolutely interesting to read."—*Gas World.*

"The volume contains a great quantity of specialised information, compiled, we believe, from trustworthy sources, which should make it of considerable value to those for whom it is specifically produced."—*Engineer.*

LIGHTING BY ACETYLENE

Generators, Burners, and Electric Furnaces. By WILLIAM E. GIBBS, M.E. With 66 Illustrations. Crown 8vo, cloth **7/6**

ENGINEERING CHEMISTRY.

A Practical Treatise for the Use of Analytical Chemists, Engineers, Iron Masters, Iron Founders, Students and others. Comprising Methods of Analysis and Valuation of the Principal Materials used in Engineering Work, with numerous Analyses, Examples and Suggestions. By H. JOSHUA PHILLIPS, F.I.C., F.C.S. Third Edition, Revised and Enlarged. Crown 8vo, 420 pp., with Plates and other Illustrations, cloth. . . . . *Net* **10/6**

"In this work the author has rendered no small service to a numerous body of practical men. . . . The analytical methods may be pronounced most satisfactory, being as accurate as the despatch required of engineering chemists permits."—*Chemical News.*

"The analytical methods given are, as a whole, such as are likely to give rapid and trustworthy results in experienced hands. . . . There is much excellent descriptive matter in the work, the chapter on 'Oils and Lubrication' being specially noticeable in this respect."—*Engineer.*

NITRO-EXPLOSIVES.

A Practical Treatise concerning the Properties, Manufacture, and Analysis of Nitrated Substances, including the Fulminates, Smokeless Powders, and Celluloid. By P. GERALD SANFORD, F.I.C., Consulting Chemist to the Cotton Powder Company, Limited, &c. With Illustrations. Crown 8vo, cloth. **9/0**

"One of the very few text-books in which can be found just what is wanted. Mr. Sanford goes steadily through the whole list of explosives commonly used, he names any given explosive and tells us of what it is composed and how it is manufactured. The book is excellent."- *Engineer.*

A HANDBOOK ON MODERN EXPLOSIVES.

A Practical Treatise on the Manufacture and Use of Dynamite, Gun-Cotton, Nitro-Glycerine and other Explosive Compounds, including Collodion-Cotton. With Chapters on Explosives in Practical Application. By M. EISSLER, M.E. Second Edition, Enlarged. Crown 8vo, cloth **12/6**

"A veritable mine of information on the subject of explosives employed for military, mining and blasting purposes."—*Army and Navy Gazette.*

A MANUAL OF THE ALKALI TRADE.

Including the Manufacture of Sulphuric Acid, Sulphate of Soda, and Bleaching Powder. By JOHN LOMAS, Alkali Manufacturer. With 232 Illustrations and Working Drawings, Second Edition, with Additions. Super-royal 8vo, cloth . . . . **£1 10s.**

"We find not merely a sound and luminous explanation of the chemical principles of the trade, but a notice of numerous matters which have a most important bearing on the successful conduct of alkali works, but which are generally overlooked by even experienced technological authors."—*Chemical Review.*

DANGEROUS GOODS.

Their Sources and Properties, Modes of Storage and Transport. With Notes and Comments on Accidents arising therefrom. A Guide for the Use of Government and Railway Officials, Steamship Owners, &c. By H. JOSHUA PHILLIPS, F.I.C., F.C.S. Crown 8vo, 374 pp., cloth **9/0**

"Merits a wide circulation, and an intelligent, appreciative study."—*Chemical News.*

THE BLOWPIPE IN CHEMISTRY, MINERALOGY, Etc.

Containing all known Methods of Anhydrous Analysis, many Working Examples, and Instructions for Making Apparatus. By Lieut.-Colonel W. A. Ross, R.A., F.G.S. Second Edition, Enlarged. Crown 8vo, cloth . **5/0**

"The student who goes conscientiously through the course of experimentation here laid down will gain a better insight into inorganic chemistry and mineralogy than if he had 'got up' any of the best text-books of the day, and passed any number of examinations in their contents."—*Chemical News.*

THE MANUAL OF COLOURS AND DYE-WARES.

Their Properties, Applications, Valuations, Impurities and Sophistications. For the Use of Dyers, Printers, Drysalters, Brokers, &c. By J. W. SLATER. Second Edition, Revised and greatly Enlarged. Crown 8vo, cloth . **7/6**

"There is no other work which covers precisely the same ground. To students preparing for examinations in dyeing and printing it will prove exceedingly useful."—*Chemical News.*

A HANDY BOOK FOR BREWERS.

Being a Practical Guide to the Art of Brewing and Malting. Embracing the Conclusions of Modern Research which bear upon the Practice of Brewing. By HERBERT EDWARDS WRIGHT, M.A. Second Edition, Enlarged. Crown 8vo, 530 pp., cloth **12/6**

"May be consulted with advantage by the student who is preparing himself for examinational tests, while the scientific brewer will find in it a *résumé* of all the most important discoveries of modern times. The work is written throughout in a clear and concise manner, and the author takes great care to discriminate between vague theories and well-established facts."—*Brewers' Journal.*

"We have great pleasure in recommending this handy book, and have no hesitation in saying that it is one of the best—if not the best—which has yet been written on the subject of beer-brewing in this country; it should have a place on the shelves of every brewer's library."—*Brewers' Guardian.*

FUELS: SOLID, LIQUID, AND GASEOUS.

Their Analysis and Valuation. For the Use of Chemists and Engineers. By H. J. PHILLIPS, F.C.S., formerly Analytical and Consulting Chemist to the G.E. Rlwy. Fourth Edition. Crown 8vo, cloth **2/0**

"Ought to have its place in the laboratory of every metallurgical establishment and wherever fuel is used on a large scale."—*Chemical News.*

THE ARTISTS' MANUAL OF PIGMENTS.

Showing their Composition, Conditions of Permanency, Non-Permanency, and Adulterations, &c., with Tests of Purity. By H. C. STANDAGE. Third Edition. Crown 8vo, cloth **2/6**

"This work is indeed *multum-in-parvo*, and we can, with good conscience, recommend it to all who come in contact with pigments, whether as makers, dealers, or users."—*Chemical Review.*

A POCKET-BOOK OF MENSURATION AND GAUGING.

Containing Tables, Rules, and Memoranda for Revenue Officers, Brewers, Spirit Merchants, &c. By J. B. MANT, Inland Revenue. Second Edition, Revised. 18mo, leather **4/0**

"Should be in the hands of every practical brewer."—*Brewers' Journal.*

INDUSTRIAL ARTS, TRADES, AND MANUFACTURES.

TEA MACHINERY AND TEA FACTORIES.

A Descriptive Treatise on the Mechanical Appliances required in the Cultivation of the Tea Plant and the Preparation of Tea for the Market. By A. J. WALLIS-TAYLER, A. M. Inst. C.E. Medium 8vo, 468 pp. With 218 Illustrations . . . . *Net* **25/0**

SUMMARY OF CONTENTS.

MECHANICAL CULTIVATION OR TILLAGE OF THE SOIL.—PLUCKING OR GATHERING THE LEAF.—TEA FACTORIES.—THE DRESSING, MANUFACTURE, OR PREPARATION OF TEA BY MECHANICAL MEANS.—ARTIFICIAL WITHERING OF THE LEAF.—MACHINES FOR ROLLING OR CURLING THE LEAF.—FERMENTING PROCESS.—MACHINES FOR THE AUTOMATIC DRYING OR FIRING OF THE LEAF.—MACHINES FOR NON-AUTOMATIC DRYING OR FIRING OF THE LEAF.—DRYING OR FIRING MACHINES.—BREAKING OR CUTTING, AND SORTING MACHINES.—PACKING THE TEA.—MEANS OF TRANSPORT ON TEA PLANTATIONS.—MISCELLANEOUS MACHINERY AND APPARATUS.—FINAL TREATMENT OF THE TEA.—TABLES AND MEMORANDA.

"The subject of tea machinery is now one of the first interest to a large class of people, to whom we strongly commend the volume."—*Chamber of Commerce Journal.*

"When tea planting was first introduced into the British possessions little, if any, machinery was employed, but now its use is almost universal. This volume contains a very full account of the machinery necessary for the proper outfit of a factory, and also a description of the processes best carried out by this machinery."—*Journal Society of Arts.*

FLOUR MANUFACTURE.

A Treatise on Milling Science and Practice. By FRIEDRICH KICK, Imperial Regierungsrath, Professor of Mechanical Technology in the Imperial German Polytechnic Institute, Prague. Translated from the Second Enlarged and Revised Edition with Supplement. By H. H. P. POWLES, Assoc. Memb. Institution of Civil Engineers. Nearly 400 pp. Illustrated with 28 Folding Plates, and 167 Woodcuts. Royal 8vo, cloth . . . . . **£1 5s.**

"This invaluable work is, and will remain, the standard authority on the science of milling. . . . The miller who has read and digested this work will have laid the foundation, so to speak, of a successful career; he will have acquired a number of general principles which he can proceed to apply. In this handsome volume we at last have the accepted text-book of modern milling in good, sound English, which has little, if any, trace of the German idiom."—*The Miller.*

"The appearance of this celebrated work in English is very opportune, and British millers will, we are sure, not be slow in availing themselves of its pages."—*Millers' Gazette.*

COTTON MANUFACTURE.

A Manual of Practical Instruction of the Processes of Opening, Carding, Combing, Drawing, Doubling and Spinning of Cotton, the Methods of Dyeing, &c. For the Use of Operatives, Overlookers, and Manufacturers. By JOHN LISTER, Technical Instructor, Pendleton. 8vo, cloth . . **7/6**

"This invaluable volume is a distinct advance in the literature of cotton manufacture."—*Machinery.*

"It is thoroughly reliable, fulfilling nearly all the requirements desired."—*Glasgow Herald.*

MODERN CYCLES.

A Practical Handbook on their Construction and Repair. By A. J. WALLIS-TAYLER, A. M. Inst. C. E., Author of "Refrigerating Machinery," &c. With upwards of 300 Illustrations. Crown 8vo, cloth **10/6**

"The large trade that is done in the component parts of bicycles has placed in the way of men mechanically inclined extraordinary facilities for building bicycles for their own use. . . . The book will prove a valuable guide for all those who aspire to the manufacture or repair of their own machines."—*The Field.*

"A most comprehensive and up-to-date treatise."—*The Cycle.*

"A very useful book, which is quite entitled to rank as a standard work for students of cycle construction."—*Wheeling.*

MOTOR CARS OR POWER CARRIAGES FOR COMMON ROADS.

By A. J. WALLIS-TAYLER, Assoc. Memb. Inst. C.E., Author of "Modern Cycles," &c. 212 pp., with 76 Illustrations. Crown 8vo, cloth . . **4/6**

"The book is clearly expressed throughout, and is just the sort of work that an engineer, thinking of turning his attention to motor-carriage work, would do well to read as a preliminary to starting operations."—*Engineering.*

PRACTICAL TANNING.

A Handbook of Modern Processes, Receipts, and Suggestions for the Treatment of Hides, Skins, and Pelts of every Description. By L. A. FLEMMING, American Tanner. 472 pages. 8vo, cloth. [*Just Published.* *Net* **25/0**

THE ART OF LEATHER MANUFACTURE.

Being a Practical Handbook, in which the Operations of Tanning, Currying, and Leather Dressing are fully Described, and the Principles of Tanning Explained, and many Recent Processes Introduced ; as also Methods for the Estimation of Tannin, and a Description of the Arts of Glue Boiling, Gut Dressing, &c. By ALEXANDER WATT. Fourth Edition. Crown 8vo cloth.
9/0

"A sound, comprehensive treatise on tanning and its accessories. The book is an eminently valuable production, which redounds to the credit of both author and publishers."—*Chemical Review.*

THE ART OF SOAP-MAKING.

A Practical Handbook of the Manufacture of Hard and Soft Soaps, Toilet Soaps, &c. Including many New Processes, and a Chapter on the Recovery of Glycerine from Waste Leys. By ALEXANDER WATT. Sixth Edition, including an Appendix on Modern Candlemaking. Crown 8vo, cloth . **7/6**

"The work will prove very useful, not merely to the technological student, but to the practical soap boiler who wishes to understand the theory of his art."—*Chemical News.*
"A thoroughly practical treatise. We congratulate the author on the success of his endeavour to fill a void in English technical literature."—*Nature.*

PRACTICAL PAPER-MAKING.

A Manual for Paper-Makers and Owners and Managers of Paper-Mills. With Tables, Calculations, &c. By G. CLAPPERTON, Paper-Maker. With Illustrations of Fibres from Micro-Photographs. Crown 8vo, cloth . . **5/0**

"The author caters for the requirements of responsible mill hands, apprentices, &c., whilst his manual will be found of great service to students of technology, as well as to veteran paper-makers and mill owners. The illustrations form an excellent feature."—*The World's Paper Trade Review.*

THE ART OF PAPER-MAKING.

A Practical Handbook of the Manufacture of Paper from Rags, Esparto, Straw, and other Fibrous Materials. Including the Manufacture of Pulp from Wood Fibre, with a Description of the Machinery and Appliances used. To which are added Details of Processes for Recovering Soda from Waste Liquors. By ALEXANDER WATT. With Illustrations. Crown 8vo, cloth . . **7/6**

"It may be regarded as the standard work on the subject. The book is full of valuable information. The 'Art of Paper-Making' is in every respect a model of a text-book, either for a technical class, or for the private student."—*Paper and Printing Trades Journal.*

A TREATISE ON PAPER.

For Printers and Stationers. With an Outline of Paper Manufacture ; Complete Tables of Sizes, and Specimens of Different Kinds of Paper. By RICHARD PARKINSON, late of the Manchester Technical School. Demy 8vo, cloth **3/6**

CEMENTS, PASTES, GLUES, AND GUMS.

A Practical Guide to the Manufacture and Application of the various Agglutinants required in the Building, Metal-Working, Wood-Working, and Leather-Working Trades, and for Workshop and Office Use. With upwards of 900 Recipes. By H. C. STANDAGE. Third Edition. Crown 8vo, cloth . **2/0**

"We have pleasure in speaking favourably of this volume. So far as we have had experience, which is not inconsiderable, this manual is trustworthy."—*Athenæum.*

THE CABINET-MAKER'S GUIDE
TO THE ENTIRE CONSTRUCTION OF CABINET WORK.

Including Veneering, Marquetrie, Buhlwork, Mosaic, Inlaying, &c. By RICHARD BITMEAD. Illustrated with Plans, Sections, and Working Drawings. Small crown 8vo, cloth **2.6**

FRENCH POLISHING AND ENAMELLING.

A Practical Work of Instruction. Including Numerous Recipes for making Polishes, Varnishes, Glaze-Lacquers, Revivers, &c. By RICHARD BITMEAD, Author of "The Cabinet-Maker's Guide." Small crown 8vo, cloth . **1 6**

WATCH REPAIRING, CLEANING, AND ADJUSTING.

A Practical Handbook dealing with the Materials and Tools Used, and the Methods of Repairing, Cleaning, Altering, and Adjusting all kinds of English and Foreign Watches, Repeaters, Chronographs, and Marine Chronometers. By F. J. GARRARD, Springer and Adjuster of Marine Chronometers and Deck Watches for the Admiralty. With over 200 Illustrations. Crown 8vo, cloth.
[Just Published. Net **4/6**

MODERN HOROLOGY, IN THEORY AND PRACTICE.

Translated from the French of CLAUDIUS SAUNIER, ex-Director of the School of Horology at Macon, by JULIEN TRIPPLIN, F.R.A.S., Besançon Watch Manufacturer, and EDWARD RIGG, M.A., Assayer in the Royal Mint. With Seventy-eight Woodcuts and Twenty-two Coloured Copper Plates. Second Edition. Super-royal 8vo, **£2 2s.**, cloth ; half-calf . . . **£2 10s.**

" There is no horological work in the English language at all to be compared to this production of M. Saunier's for clearness and completeness. It is alike good as a guide for the student and as a reference for the experienced horologist and skilled workman."—*Horological Journal.*
" The latest, the most complete, and the most reliable of those literary productions to which continental watchmakers are indebted for the mechanical superiority over their English brethren —in fact, the Book of Books is M. Saunier's ' Treatise.'"—*Watchmaker, Jeweller, and Silversmith.*

THE WATCH ADJUSTER'S MANUAL.

A Practical Guide for the Watch and Chronometer Adjuster in Making, Springing, Timing and Adjusting for Isochronism, Positions and Temperatures. By C. E. FRITTS. 370 pp., with Illustrations, 8vo, cloth . . . **16/0**

THE WATCHMAKER'S HANDBOOK.

Intended as a Workshop Companion for those engaged in Watchmaking and the Allied Mechanical Arts. Translated from the French of CLAUDIUS SAUNIER, and enlarged by JULIEN TRIPPLIN, F.R.A.S., and EDWARD RIGG, M.A., Assayer in the Royal Mint. Third Edition. Cr. 8vo, cloth. . **9/0**

" Each part is truly a treatise in itself. The arrangement is good and the language is clear and concise. It is an admirable guide for the young watchmaker."—*Engineering.*

HISTORY OF WATCHES & OTHER TIMEKEEPERS.

By JAMES F. KENDAL, M.B.H. Inst. **1 6** boards; or cloth, gilt . **2/6**

" The best which has yet appeared on this subject in the English language."—*Industries.*
" Open the book where you may, there is interesting matter in it concerning the ingenious devices of the ancient or modern horologer."—*Saturday Review.*

ELECTRO-PLATING & ELECTRO-REFINING OF METALS.

Being a new edition of ALEXANDER WATT's "ELECTRO-DEPOSITION." Revised and Largely Rewritten by ARNOLD PHILIP, B.Sc., A.I.E.E., Principal Assistant to the Admiralty Chemist. Large Crown 8vo, cloth. . Net **12 6**

" Altogether the work can be highly recommended to every electro-plater, and is of undoubted interest to every electro-metallurgist."—*Electrical Review.*
" Eminently a book for the practical worker in electro-deposition. It contains practical descriptions of methods, processes and materials, as actually pursued and used in the workshop."— *Engineer.*

ELECTRO-METALLURGY.

Practically Treated. By ALEXANDER WATT. Tenth Edition, including the most recent Processes. 12mo, cloth **3/6**

" From this book both amateur and artisan may learn everything necessary for the successful prosecution of electroplating."—*Iron.*

JEWELLER'S ASSISTANT IN WORKING IN GOLD.

A Practical Treatise for Masters and Workmen, Compiled from the Experience of Thirty Years' Workshop Practice. By GEORGE E. GEE. Crown 8vo. **7/6**

" This manual of technical education is apparently destined to be a valuable auxiliary to a handicraft which is certainly capable of great improvement."—*The Times.*

ELECTROPLATING.

A Practical Handbook on the Deposition of Copper, Silver, Nickel, Gold, Aluminium, Brass, Platinum, &c., &c. By J. W. URQUHART, C.E. Fourth Edition, Revised. Crown 8vo, cloth **5/0**

" An excellent practical manual."—*Engineering.*
" An excellent work, giving the newest information."—*Horological Journal.*

ELECTROTYPING.

The Reproduction and Multiplication of Printing Surfaces and Works of Art by the Electro-Deposition of Metals. By J. W. URQUHART, C.E. Crown 8vo, cloth **5/0**

"The book is thoroughly practical; the reader is, therefore, conducted through the leading laws of electricity, then through the metals used by electrotypers, the apparatus, and the depositing processes, up to the final preparation of the work."—*Art Journal.*

GOLDSMITH'S HANDBOOK.

By GEORGE E. GEE, Jeweller, &c. Fifth Edition. 12mo, cloth . . **3/0**

"A good, sound educator."—*Horological Journal.*

SILVERSMITH'S HANDBOOK.

By GEORGE E. GEE, Jeweller, &c. Third Edition, with numerous Illustrations. 12mo, cloth **3/0**

"The chief merit of the work is its practical character. . . . The workers in the trade will speedily discover its merits when they sit down to study it."—*English Mechanic.*

*** *The above two works together, strongly half-bound, price 7s.*

SHEET METAL WORKER'S INSTRUCTOR.

Comprising a Selection of Geometrical Problems and Practical Rules for Describing the Various Patterns Required by Zinc, Sheet-Iron, Copper, and Tin-Plate Workers. By REUBEN HENRY WARN, Practical Tin-Plate Worker. New Edition, Revised and greatly Enlarged by JOSEPH G. HORNER, A.M.I.M.E. Crown 8vo, 254 pp., with 430 Illustrations, cloth . . **7/6**

SAVOURIES AND SWEETS

Suitable for Luncheons and Dinners. By Miss M L. ALLEN (Mrs. A. MACAIRE), Author of "Breakfast Dishes," &c. Twenty-ninth Edition. F'cap 8vo, sewed **1/0**

BREAKFAST DISHES

For Every Morning of Three Months. By Miss ALLEN (Mrs A. MACAIRE), Author of "Savouries and Sweets," &c. Twenty-second Edition. F'cap 8vo, sewed **1/0**

BREAD & BISCUIT BAKER'S & SUGAR-BOILER'S ASSISTANT.

Including a large variety of Modern Recipes. With Remarks on the Art of Bread-making. By ROBERT WELLS. Third Edition. Crown 8vo . . **1/0**

"A large number of wrinkles for the ordinary cook, as well as the baker."—*Saturday Review.*

PASTRYCOOK & CONFECTIONER'S GUIDE.

For Hotels, Restaurants, and the Trade in general, adapted also for Family Use. By R. WELLS, Author of "The Bread and Biscuit Baker " . . **1/0**

"We cannot speak too highly of this really excellent work. In these days of keen competition our readers cannot do better than purchase this book."—*Bakers' Times.*

ORNAMENTAL CONFECTIONERY.

A Guide for Bakers, Confectioners and Pastrycooks; including a variety of Modern Recipes, and Remarks on Decorative and Coloured Work. With 129 Original Designs. By ROBERT WELLS. Crown 8vo, cloth . . . **5/0**

"A valuable work, practical, and should be in the hands of every baker and confectioner. The illustrative designs are worth treble the amount charged for the work."—*Bakers' Times.*

MODERN FLOUR CONFECTIONER.

Containing a large Collection of Recipes for Cheap Cakes, Biscuits, &c. With remarks on the Ingredients Used in their Manufacture. By R. WELLS. **1/0**

"The work is of a decidedly practical character, and in every recipe regard is had to economical working.'—*North British Daily Mail.*

RUBBER HAND STAMPS

And the Manipulation of Rubber. A Practical Treatise on the Manufacture of Indiarubber Hand Stamps, Small Articles of Indiarubber, The Hektograph, Special Inks, Cements, and Allied Subjects. By T. O'CONOR SLOANE, A.M., Ph.D. With numerous Illustrations. Square 8vo, cloth. . . . **5/0**

HANDYBOOKS FOR HANDICRAFTS.

BY PAUL N. HASLUCK.

Editor of " Work " (New Series), Author of " Lathe Work," " Milling Machines," &c.
Crown 8vo, 144 pp., price 1s. each.

☞ *These* HANDYBOOKS *have been written to supply information for* WORKMEN, STUDENTS, *and* AMATEURS *in the several Handicrafts, on the actual* PRACTICE *of the* WORKSHOP, *and are intended to convey in plain language* TECHNICAL KNOW-LEDGE *of the several* CRAFTS." *In describing the processes employed, and the manipulation of material, workshop terms are used ; workshop practice is fully explained ; and the text is freely illustrated with drawings of modern tools, appliances, and processes.*

METAL TURNER'S HANDYBOOK.

A Practical Manual for Workers at the Foot-Lathe. With 100 Illustrations.
1/0

" The book will be of service alike to the amateur and the artisan turner. It displays thorough knowledge of the subject."—*Scotsman.*

WOOD TURNER'S HANDYBOOK.

A Practical Manual for Workers at the Lathe. With over 100 Illustrations.
1/0

" We recommend the book to young turners and amateurs. A multitude of workmen have hitherto sought in vain for a manual of this special industry."—*Mechanical World.*

WATCH JOBBER'S HANDYBOOK.

A Practical Manual on Cleaning, Repairing, and Adjusting. With upwards of 100 Illustrations **1/0**
" We strongly advise all young persons connected with the watch trade to acquire and study this inexpensive work."—*Clerkenwell Chronicle.*

PATTERN MAKER'S HANDYBOOK.

A Practical Manual on the Construction of Patterns for Founders. With upwards of 100 Illustrations **1/0**
" A most valuable, if not indispensable manual for the pattern maker."—*Knowledge.*

MECHANIC'S WORKSHOP HANDYBOOK.

A Practical Manual on Mechanical Manipulation, embracing Information on various Handicraft Processes. With Useful Notes and Miscellaneous Memoranda. Comprising about 200 Subjects **1/0**
" A very clever and useful book, which should be found in every workshop; and it should certainly find a place in all technical schools."—*Saturday Review.*

MODEL ENGINEER'S HANDYBOOK.

A Practical Manual on the Construction of Model Steam Engines. With upwards of 100 Illustrations. **1/0**
" Mr. Hasluck has produced a very good little book."—*Builder.*

CLOCK JOBBER'S HANDYBOOK.

A Practical Manual on Cleaning, Repairing, and Adjusting. With upwards of 100 Illustrations **1/0**
" It is of inestimable service to those commencing the trade."—*Coventry Standard.*

CABINET WORKER'S HANDYBOOK.

A Practical Manual on the Tools, Materials, Appliances, and Processes employed in Cabinet Work. With upwards of 100 Illustrations . . **1/0**
" Mr. Hasluck's thorough-going little Handybook is amongst the most practical guides we have seen for beginners in cabinet-work."—*Saturday Review.*

WOODWORKER'S HANDYBOOK.

Embracing Information on the Tools, Materials, Appliances and Processes Employed in Woodworking. With 104 Illustrations. . . . **1/0**
" Written by a man who knows, not only how work ought to be done, but how to do it, and how to convey his knowledge to others. '—*Engineering.*
" Mr. Hasluck writes admirably, and gives complete instructions."—*Engineer.*
" Mr. Hasluck combines the experience of a practical teacher with the manipulative skill and scientific knowledge of processes of the trained mechanician, and the manuals are marvels of what can be produced at a popular price."—*Schoolmaster.*
" Helpful to workmen of all ages and degrees of experience."—*Daily Chronicle*
" Concise, clear, and practical."—*Saturday Review.*

COMMERCE, COUNTING-HOUSE WORK, TABLES, ETC.

LESSONS IN COMMERCE.

By Professor R. GAMBARO, of the Royal High Commercial School at Genoa. Edited and Revised by JAMES GAULT, Professor of Commerce and Commercial Law in King's College, London. Fourth Edition. Crown 8vo, cloth . **3/6**

" The publishers of this work have rendered considerable service to the cause of commercial education by the opportune production of this volume. . . . The work is peculiarly acceptable to English readers and an admirable addition to existing class books. In a phrase, we think the work attains its object in furnishing a brief account of those laws and customs of British trade with which the commercial man interested therein should be familiar."—*Chamber of Commerce Journal.*

" An invaluable guide in the hands of those who are preparing for a commercial career, and, in fact, the information it contains on matters of business should be impressed on every one."—*Counting House.*

THE FOREIGN COMMERCIAL CORRESPONDENT.

Being Aids to Commercial Correspondence in Five Languages—English, French, German, Italian, and Spanish. By CONRAD E. BAKER. Third Edition, Carefully Revised Throughout. Crown 8vo, cloth . . **4/6**

" Whoever wishes to correspond in all the languages mentioned by Mr. Baker cannot do better than study this work, the materials of which are excellent and conveniently arranged They consist not of entire specimen letters, but—what are far more useful—short passages, sentences, or phrases expressing the same general idea in various forms."—*Athenæum.*

" A careful examination has convinced us that it is unusually complete, well arranged and reliable. The book is a thoroughly good one."—*Schoolmaster.*

FACTORY ACCOUNTS: their PRINCIPLES & PRACTICE.

A Handbook for Accountants and Manufacturers, with Appendices on the Nomenclature of Machine Details; the Income Tax Acts; the Rating of Factories; Fire and Boiler Insurance; the Factory and Workshop Acts, &c., including also a Glossary of Terms and a large number of Specimen Rulings. By EMILE GARCKE and J. M. FELLS. Fifth Edition, Revised and Enlarged. Demy 8vo, cloth **7/6**

" A very interesting description of the requirements of Factory Accounts. . . . The principle of assimilating the Factory Accounts to the general commercial books is one which we thoroughly agree with."—*Accountants' Journal.*

" Characterised by extreme thoroughness. There are few owners of factories who would not derive great benefit from the perusal of this most admirable work."—*Local Government Chronicle.*

MODERN METROLOGY.

A Manual of the Metrical Units and Systems of the present Century. With an Appendix containing a proposed English System. By LOWIS D. A. JACKSON, A. M. Inst. C. E., Author of " Aid to Survey Practice," &c. Large crown 8vo, cloth **12/6**

" We recommend the work to all interested in the practical reform of our weights and measures."—*Nature.*

A SERIES OF METRIC TABLES.

In which the British Standard Measures and Weights are compared with those of the Metric System at present in Use on the Continent. By C. H. DOWLING, C.E. 8vo, cloth **10/6**

" Mr. Dowling's Tables are well put together as a ready reckoner for the conversion of one system into the other."—*Athenæum.*

IRON AND METAL TRADES' COMPANION.

For Expeditiously Ascertaining the Value of any Goods bought or sold by Weight, from 1s. per cwt. to 112s. per cwt., and from one farthing per pound to one shilling per pound. By THOMAS DOWNIE. Strongly bound in leather, 396 pp. **9/0**

" A most useful set of tables, nothing like them before existed."—*Building News.*

" Although specially adapted to the iron and metal trades, the tables will be found useful every other business in which merchandise is bought and sold by weight."—*Railway News.*

NUMBER, WEIGHT, AND FRACTIONAL CALCULATOR.

Containing upwards of 250,000 Separate Calculations, showing at a Glance the Value at 422 Different Rates, ranging from $\frac{1}{16}$th of a Penny to 20s. each, or per cwt., and £20 per ton, of any number of articles consecutively, from 1 to 470. Any number of cwts., qrs., and lbs., from 1 cwt. to 470 cwts. Any number of tons, cwts., qrs., and lbs., from 1 to 1,000 tons. By WILLIAM CHADWICK, Public Accountant. Third Edition, Revised and Improved. 8vo, strongly bound **18/0**

" It is as easy of reference for any answer or any number of answers as a dictionary. For making up accounts or estimates the book must prove invaluable to all who have any considerable quantity of calculations involving price and measure in any combination to do."—*Engineer.*
"The most perfect work of the kind yet prepared."—*Glasgow Herald.*

THE WEIGHT CALCULATOR.

Being a Series of Tables upon a New and Comprehensive Plan, exhibiting at one Reference the exact Value of any Weight from 1 lb. to 15 tons, at 300 Progressive Rates, from 1d. to 168s. per cwt., and containing 186,000 Direct Answers, which, with their Combinations, consisting of a single addition (mostly to be performed at sight), will afford an aggregate of 10,266,000 Answers ; the whole being calculated and designed to ensure correctness and promote despatch. By HENRY HARBEN, Accountant. Sixth Edition, carefully Corrected. Royal 8vo, strongly half-bound.   *[Just Published.* **£1 5s.**

" A practical and useful work of reference for men of business generally."—*Ironmonger.*
"Of priceless value to business men. It is a necessary book in all mercantile offices."—*Sheffield Independent.*

THE DISCOUNT GUIDE.

Comprising several Series of Tables for the Use of Merchants, Manufacturers, Ironmongers, and Others, by which may be ascertained the Exact Profit arising from any mode of using Discounts, either in the Purchase or Sale of Goods, and the method of either Altering a Rate of Discount, or Advancing a Price, so as to produce, by one operation, a sum that will realise any required Profit after allowing one or more Discounts : to which are added Tables of Profit or Advance from 1¼ to 90 per cent., Tables of Discount from 1¼ to 98¾ per cent., and Tables of Commission, &c., from ⅛ to 10 per cent. By HENRY HARBEN, Accountant. New Edition, Corrected. Demy 8vo, half-bound . **£1 5s.**

" A book such as this can only be appreciated by business men, to whom the saving of time means saving of money. The work must prove of great value to merchants, manufacturers, and general traders."—*British Trade Journal.*

TABLES OF WAGES.

At 54, 52, 50 and 48 Hours per Week. Showing the Amounts of Wages from One quarter of an hour to Sixty-four hours, in each case at Rates of Wages advancing by One Shilling from 4s. to 55s. per week. By THOS. GARBUTT, Accountant. Square crown 8vo, half-bound **6/0**

IRON-PLATE WEIGHT TABLES.

For Iron Shipbuilders, Engineers, and Iron Merchants. Containing the Calculated Weights of upwards of 150,000 different sizes of Iron Plates from 1 foot by 6 in. by ¼ in. to 10 feet by 5 feet by 1 in. Worked out on the Basis of 40 lbs. to the square foot of Iron of 1 inch in thickness. By H. BURLINSON and W. H. SIMPSON. 4to, half-bound . . . . . . **£1 5s.**

AGRICULTURE, FARMING, GARDENING, ETC.

THE COMPLETE GRAZIER AND FARMER'S AND CATTLE BREEDER'S ASSISTANT.

A Compendium of Husbandry. Originally Written by WILLIAM YOUATT. Fourteenth Edition, entirely Re-written, considerably Enlarged, and brought up to Present Requirements, by WILLIAM FREAM, LL.D., Assistant Commissioner, Royal Commission on Agriculture, Author of "The Elements of Agriculture," &c. Royal 8vo, 1,100 pp., 450 Illustrations, handsomely bound.

£1 11s. 6D.

BOOK I. ON THE VARIETIES, BREEDING, REARING, FATTENING AND MANAGEMENT OF CATTLE.
BOOK II. ON THE ECONOMY AND MANAGEMENT OF THE DAIRY.
BOOK III. ON THE BREEDING, REARING, AND MANAGEMENT OF HORSES.
BOOK IV. ON THE BREEDING, REARING, AND FATTENING OF SHEEP.
BOOK V. ON THE BREEDING, REARING, AND FATTENING OF SWINE.
BOOK VI. ON THE DISEASES OF LIVE STOCK.

BOOK VII. ON THE BREEDING, REARING, AND MANAGEMENT OF POULTRY.
BOOK VIII. ON FARM OFFICES AND IMPLEMENTS OF HUSBANDRY.
BOOK IX. ON THE CULTURE AND MANAGEMENT OF GRASS LANDS.
BOOK X. ON THE CULTIVATION AND APPLICATION OF GRASSES, PULSE AND ROOTS.
BOOK XI. ON MANURES AND THEIR APPLICATION TO GRASS LAND AND CROPS.
BOOK XII. MONTHLY CALENDARS OF FARMWORK.

"Dr. Fream is to be congratulated on the successful attempt he has made to give us a work which will at once become the standard classic of the farm practice of the country. We believe that it will be found that it has no compeer among the many works at present in existence. . . . The illustrations are admirable, while the frontispiece, which represents the well-known bull, New Year's Gift, bred by the Queen, is a work of art."—*The Times.*

"The book must be recognised as occupying the proud position of the most exhaustive work of reference in the English language on the subject with which it deals."—*Athenæum.*

"The most comprehensive guide to modern farm practice that exists in the English language to-day . . . The book is one that ought to be on every farm and in the library of every land owner."—*Mark Lane Express.*

"In point of exhaustiveness and accuracy the work will certainly hold a pre-eminent and unique position among books dealing with scientific agricultural practice. It is, in fact, an agricultural library of itself."—*North British Agriculturist.*

FARM LIVE STOCK OF GREAT BRITAIN.

BY ROBERT WALLACE, F.L.S., F.R.S.E., &c., Professor of Agriculture and Rural Economy in the University of Edinburgh. Third Edition, thoroughly Revised and considerably Enlarged. With over 120 Phototypes of Prize Stock. Demy 8vo, 384 pp., with 79 Plates and Maps, cloth. . . 12/6

"A really complete work on the history, breeds, and management of the farm stock of Great Britain, and one which is likely to find its way to the shelves of every country gentleman's library."—*The Times.*

"The 'Farm Live Stock of Great Britain' is a production to be proud of, and its issue not the least of the services which its author has rendered to agricultural science."—*Scottish Farmer.*

NOTE-BOOK OF AGRICULTURAL FACTS & FIGURES FOR FARMERS AND FARM STUDENTS.

By PRIMROSE McCONNELL, B.Sc., Fellow of the Highland and Agricultural Society, Author of "Elements of Farming." Sixth Edition, Re-written, Revised, and greatly Enlarged. Fcap. 8vo, 480 pp., leather, gilt edges . . 6/0

CONTENTS.—SURVEYING AND LEVELLING.—WEIGHTS AND MEASURES.—MACHINERY AND BUILDINGS. — LABOUR. — OPERATIONS. — DRAINING. — EMBANKING. — GEOLOGICAL MEMORANDA. — SOILS. — MANURES. — CROPPING. — CROPS.—ROTATIONS. — WEEDS. — FEEDING.—DAIRYING.—LIVE STOCK.—HORSES.— CATTLE. — SHEEP.—PIGS.—POULTRY.—FORESTRY.—HORTICULTURE.—MISCELLANEOUS.

"No farmer, and certainly no agricultural student, ought to be without this *multum-in-parvo* manual of all subjects connected with the farm."—*North British Agriculturist.*

"This little pocket-book contains a large amount of useful information upon all kinds of agricultural subjects. Something of the kind has long been wanted."—*Mark Lane Express.*

"The amount of information it contains is most surprising; the arrangement of the matter is so methodical—although so compressed—as to be intelligible to everyone who takes a glance through its pages. They teem with information."—*Farm and Home.*

THE ELEMENTS OF AGRICULTURAL GEOLOGY.

A Scientific Aid to Practical Farming. By PRIMROSE McCONNELL. Author of "Note-Book of Agricultural Facts and Figures," &c. Royal 8vo, cloth.

Net 21/0

"On every page the work bears the impress of a masterly knowledge of the subject dealt with, and we have nothing but unstinted praise to offer."—*Field.*

BRITISH DAIRYING.

A Handy Volume on the Work of the Dairy-Farm. For the Use of Technical Instruction Classes, Students in Agricultural Colleges and the Working Dairy-Farmer. By Prof. J. P. SHELDON. With Illustrations. Second Edition, Revised. Crown 8vo, cloth **2/6**

"Confidently recommended as a useful text-book on dairy farming."—*Agricultural Gazette.*
"Probably the best half-crown manual on dairy work that has yet been produced."—*North British Agriculturist.*
"It is the soundest little work we have yet seen on the subject."—*The Times.*

MILK, CHEESE, AND BUTTER.

A Practical Handbook on their Properties and the Processes of their Production. Including a Chapter on Cream and the Methods of its Separation from Milk. By JOHN OLIVER, late Principal of the Western Dairy Institute, Berkeley. With Coloured Plates and 200 Illustrations. Crown 8vo, cloth.

7/6

"An exhaustive and masterly production. It may be cordially recommended to all students and practitioners of dairy science."—*North British Agriculturist.*
"We recommend this very comprehensive and carefully-written book to dairy-farmers and students of dairying. It is a distinct acquisition to the library of the agriculturist."—*Agricultural Gazette.*

SYSTEMATIC SMALL FARMING.

Or, The Lessons of My Farm. Being an Introduction to Modern Farm Practice for Small Farmers. By R. SCOTT BURN, Author of "Outlines of Modern Farming," &c. Crown 8vo, cloth. **6/0**

"This is the completest book of its class we have seen, and one which every amateur farmer will read with pleasure, and accept as a guide."—*Field.*

OUTLINES OF MODERN FARMING.

By R. SCOTT BURN. Soils, Manures, and Crops—Farming and Farming Economy—Cattle, Sheep, and Horses—Management of Dairy, Pigs, and Poultry—Utilisation of Town-Sewage, Irrigation, &c. Sixth Edition. In One Vol., 1,250 pp., half-bound, profusely Illustrated **12/0**

FARM ENGINEERING, The COMPLETE TEXT-BOOK of.

Comprising Draining and Embanking ; Irrigation and Water Supply ; Farm Roads, Fences and Gates ; Farm Buildings ; Barn Implements and Machines ; Field Implements and Machines ; Agricultural Surveying, &c. By Professor JOHN SCOTT. In One Vol., 1,150 pp., half-bound, with over 600 Illustrations.

12/0

"Written with great care, as well as with knowledge and ability. The author has done his work well; we have found him a very trustworthy guide wherever we have tested his statements. The volume will be of great value to agricultural students."—*Mark Lane Express.*

THE FIELDS OF GREAT BRITAIN.

A Text-Book of Agriculture. Adapted to the Syllabus of the Science and Art Department. For Elementary and Advanced Students. By HUGH CLEMENTS (Board of Trade). Second Edition, Revised, with Additions. 18mo, cloth **2/6**

"It is a long time since we have seen a book which has pleased us more, or which contains uch a vast and useful fund of knowledge."—*Educational Times*

TABLES and MEMORANDA for FARMERS, GRAZIERS, AGRICULTURAL STUDENTS, SURVEYORS, LAND AGENTS, AUCTIONEERS, &c.

With a New System of Farm Book-keeping. By SIDNEY FRANCIS. Fifth Edition. 272 pp., waistcoat-pocket size, limp leather **1/6**

"Weighing less than 1 oz., and occupying no more space than a match-box, it contains a mass of facts and calculations which has never before, in such handy form, been obtainable. Every operation on the farm is dealt with. The work may be taken as thoroughly accurate, the whole of the tables having been revised by Dr. Fream. We cordially recommend it."—*Bell's Weekly Messenger.*

THE ROTHAMSTED EXPERIMENTS AND THEIR PRACTICAL LESSONS FOR FARMERS.

Part I. STOCK. Part II. CROPS. By C. J. R. TIPPER. Crown 8vo, cloth.

3/6

"We have no doubt that the book will be welcomed by a large class of farmers and others interested in agriculture."—*Standard.*

FERTILISERS AND FEEDING STUFFS.

Their Properties and Uses. A Handbook for the Practical Farmer. By BERNARD DYER, D.Sc. (Lond.). With the Text of the Fertilisers and Feeding Stuffs Act of 1893, The Regulations and Forms of the Board of Agriculture, and Notes on the Act by A. J. DAVID, B.A., LL.M. Fourth Edition, Revised. Crown 8vo, cloth. [*Just Published.* 1/0

"This little book is precisely what it professes to be—'A Handbook for the Practical Farmer.' Dr. Dyer has done farmers good service in placing at their disposal so much useful information in so intelligible a form."—*The Times.*

BEES FOR PLEASURE AND PROFIT.

A Guide to the Manipulation of Bees, the Production of Honey, and the General Management of the Apiary. By G. GORDON SAMSON. With numerous Illustrations. Crown 8vo, wrapper 1/0

BOOK-KEEPING for FARMERS and ESTATE OWNERS.

A Practical Treatise, presenting, in Three Plans, a System adapted for all Classes of Farms. By JOHNSON M. WOODMAN, Chartered Accountant. Fourth Edition. Crown 8vo, cloth. [*Just Published.* 2/6

"The volume is a capital study of a most important subject."—*Agricultural Gazette.*

WOODMAN'S YEARLY FARM ACCOUNT BOOK.

Giving Weekly Labour Account and Diary, and showing the Income and Expenditure under each Department of Crops, Live Stock, Dairy, &c., &c. With Valuation, Profit and Loss Account, and Balance Sheet at the End of the Year. By JOHNSON M. WOODMAN, Chartered Accountant. Second Edition. Folio, half-bound . . . . *Net* 7/6

"Contains every requisite for keeping farm accounts readily and accurately."—*Agriculture.*

THE FORCING GARDEN.

Or, How to Grow Early Fruits, Flowers and Vegetables. With Plans and Estimates for Building Glasshouses, Pits and Frames. With Illustrations. By SAMUEL WOOD. Crown 8vo, cloth 3/6

"A good book, containing a great deal of valuable teaching."—*Gardeners' Magazine.*

A PLAIN GUIDE TO GOOD GARDENING.

Or, How to Grow Vegetables, Fruits, and Flowers. By S. WOOD. Fourth Edition, with considerable Additions, and numerous Illustrations. Crown 8vo, cloth 3/6

"A very good book, and one to be highly recommended as a practical guide. The practical directions are excellent."—*Athenæum.*

MULTUM-IN-PARVO GARDENING.

Or, How to Make One Acre of Land produce £620 a year, by the Cultivation of Fruits and Vegetables ; also, How to Grow Flowers in Three Glass Houses, so as to realise £176 per annum clear Profit. By SAMUEL WOOD, Author of "Good Gardening," &c. Sixth Edition, Crown 8vo, sewed . . . 1/0

THE LADIES' MULTUM-IN-PARVO FLOWER GARDEN.

And Amateur's Complete Guide. By S. WOOD. Crown 8vo, cloth . 3/6

POTATOES: HOW TO GROW AND SHOW THEM.

A Practical Guide to the Cultivation and General Treatment of the Potato. By J. PINK. Crown 8vo 2/0

MARKET AND KITCHEN GARDENING.

By C. W. SHAW, late Editor of "Gardening Illustrated." Crown 8vo, cloth. 3/6

AUCTIONEERING, VALUING, LAND SURVEYING, ESTATE AGENCY, ETC.

INWOOD'S TABLES FOR PURCHASING ESTATES
AND FOR THE VALUATION OF PROPERTIES,

Including Advowsons, Assurance Policies, Copyholds, Deferred Annuities, Freeholds, Ground Rents, Immediate Annuities, Leaseholds, Life Interests, Mortgages, Perpetuities, Renewals of Leases, Reversions, Sinking Funds, &c., &c. 27th Edition, Revised and Extended by WILLIAM SCHOOLING, F.R.A.S., with Logarithms of Natural Numbers and THOMAN's Logarithmic Interest and Annuity Tables. 360 pp., Demy 8vo, cloth.

[*Just Published.* Net **8/0**

"Those interested in the purchase and sale of estates, and in the adjustment of compensation cases, as well as in transactions in annuities, life insurances, &c., will find the present edition of eminent service."—*Engineering.*

"This valuable book has been considerably enlarged and improved by the labours of Mr. Schooling, and is now very complete indeed."—*Economist.*

"Altogether this edition will prove of extreme value to many classes of professional men in saving them many long and tedious calculations."—*Investors' Review.*

THE APPRAISER, AUCTIONEER, BROKER, HOUSE
AND ESTATE AGENT AND VALUER'S POCKET ASSISTANT.

For the Valuation for Purchase, Sale, or Renewal of Leases, Annuities, and Reversions, and of Property generally; with Prices for Inventories, &c. By JOHN WHEELER, Valuer, &c. Sixth Edition, Re-written and greatly Extended by C. NORRIS. Royal 32mo, cloth **5/0**

"A neat and concise book of reference, containing an admirable and clearly-arranged list of prices for inventories, and a very practical guide to determine the value of furniture, &c."—*Standard.*
"Contains a large quantity of varied and useful information as to the valuation for purchase, sale, or renewal of leases, annuities and reversions, and of property generally, with prices for inventories, and a guide to determine the value of interior fittings and other effects."—*Builder.*

AUCTIONEERS: THEIR DUTIES AND LIABILITIES.

A Manual of Instruction and Counsel for the Young Auctioneer. By ROBERT SQUIBBS, Auctioneer. Second Edition, Revised. Demy 8vo, cloth . **12/6**

"The work is one of general excellent character, and gives much information in a compendious and satisfactory form."—*Builder.*
"May be recommended as giving a great deal of information on the law relating to auctioneers, in a very readable form."—*Law Journal.*

THE AGRICULTURAL VALUER'S ASSISTANT.

A Practical Handbook on the Valuation of Landed Estates; including Example of a Detailed Report on Management and Realisation; Forms of Valuations of Tenant Right; Lists of Local Agricultural Customs; Scales of Compensation under the Agricultural Holdings Act, and a Brief Treatise on Compensation under the Lands Clauses Acts, &c. By TOM BRIGHT, Agricultural Valuer. Author of "The Agricultural Surveyor and Estate Agent's Handbook." Fourth Edition, Revised, with Appendix containing a Digest of the Agricultural Holdings Acts, 1883 and 1900. Crown 8vo, cloth . Net **6/0**

"Full of tables and examples in connection with the valuation of tenant-right, estates, labour, contents and weights of timber, and farm produce of all kinds."—*Agricultural Gazette.*
"An eminently practical handbook, full of practical tables and data of undoubted interest and value to surveyors and auctioneers in preparing valuations of all kinds."—*Farmer.*

POLE PLANTATIONS AND UNDERWOODS.

A Practical Handbook on Estimating the Cost of Forming, Renovating, Improving, and Grubbing Plantations and Underwoods, their Valuation for Purposes of Transfer, Rental, Sale or Assessment. By TOM BRIGHT. Crown 8vo, cloth **3/6**

"To valuers, foresters and agents it will be a welcome aid."—*North British Agriculturist.*
"Well calculated to assist the valuer in the discharge of his duties, and of undoubted interest and use both to surveyors and auctioneers in preparing valuations of all kinds."—*Kent Herald.*

AGRICULTURAL SURVEYOR AND ESTATE AGENT'S HANDBOOK.

Of Practical Rules, Formulæ, Tables, and Data. A Comprehensive Manual for the Use of Surveyors, Agents, Landowners, and others interested in the Equipment, the Management, or the Valuation of Landed Estates. By TOM BRIGHT, Agricultural Surveyor and Valuer, Author of "The Agricultural Valuer's Assistant," &c. With Illustrations. Fcap. 8vo, Leather.
Net **7/6**

"An exceedingly useful book, the contents of which are admirably chosen. The classes for whom the work is intended will find it convenient to have this comprehensive handbook accessible for reference."—*Live Stock Journal.*
"It is a singularly compact and well informed compendium of the facts and figures likely to be required in estate work, and is certain to prove of much service to those to whom it is addressed."—*Scotsman.*

THE LAND VALUER'S BEST ASSISTANT.

Being Tables on a very much Improved Plan, for Calculating the Value of Estates. With Tables for reducing Scotch, Irish, and Provincial Customary Acres to Statute Measure, &c. By R. HUDSON, C.E. New Edition. Royal 32mo, leather, elastic band **4/0**
"Of incalculable value to the country gentleman and professional man."—*Farmers' Journal.*

THE LAND IMPROVER'S POCKET-BOOK.

Comprising Formulæ, Tables, and Memoranda required in any Computation relating to the Permanent Improvement of Landed Property. By JOHN EWART, Surveyor. Second Edition, Revised. Royal 32mo, oblong, leather . **4/0**
"A compendious and handy little volume."—*Spectator.*

THE LAND VALUER'S COMPLETE POCKET-BOOK.

Being the above Two Works bound together. Leather **7/6**

HANDBOOK OF HOUSE PROPERTY.

A Popular and Practical Guide to the Purchase, Tenancy, and Compulsory Sale of Houses and Land, including Dilapidations and Fixtures: with Examples of all kinds of Valuations, Information on Building and on the right use of Decorative Art. By E. L. TARBUCK, Architect and Surveyor. Sixth Edition. 12mo, cloth **5/0**
"The advice is thoroughly practical."—*Law Journal.*
"For all who have dealings with house property, this is an indispensable guide."—*Decoration.*
"Carefully brought up to date, and much improved by the addition of a division on Fine Art. A well-written and thoughtful work."—*Land Agents' Record.*

LAW AND MISCELLANEOUS.

MODERN JOURNALISM.

A Handbook of Instruction and Counsel for the Young Journalist. By JOHN B. MACKIE, Fellow of the Institute of Journalists. Crown 8vo, cloth . **2/0**
"This invaluable guide to journalism is a work which all aspirants to a journalistic career will read with advantage."—*Journalist.*

HANDBOOK FOR SOLICITORS AND ENGINEERS

Engaged in Promoting Private Acts of Parliament and Provisional Orders for the Authorisation of Railways, Tramways, Gas and Water Works, &c. By L. L MACASSEY, of the Middle Temple, Barrister-at-Law, M.I.C.E. 8vo, cloth . . . . **£1 5s.**

PATENTS for INVENTIONS, HOW to PROCURE THEM.

Compiled for the Use of Inventors, Patentees and others. By G. G. M. HARDINGHAM, Assoc. Mem. Inst. C.E., &c. Demy 8vo, cloth . . **1/6**

CONCILIATION & ARBITRATION in LABOUR DISPUTES.

A Historical Sketch and Brief Statement of the Present Position of the Question at Home and Abroad. By J. S. JEANS. Crown 8vo, 200 pp., cloth **2/6**

EVERY MAN'S OWN LAWYER.

A Handy-Book of the Principles of Law and Equity. With a Concise Dictionary of Legal Terms. By A BARRISTER. Forty-first Edition, carefully Revised, and comprising New Acts of Parliament, including the *Motor Car Act*, 1903; *Employment of Children Act*, 1903; *Pistols Act*, 1903; *Poor Prisoners' Defence Act*, 1903; *Education Acts of 1902 and 1903*; *Housing of the Working Classes Act*, 1903, &c. *Judicial Decisions* pronounced during the year have also been duly noted. Crown 8vo, 800 pp., strongly bound in cloth.
[Just Published. **6/8**

*** *This Standard Work of Reference forms* A COMPLETE EPITOME OF THE LAWS OF ENGLAND, *comprising (amongst other matter)*:

THE RIGHTS AND WRONGS OF INDIVIDUALS

LANDLORD AND TENANT
VENDORS AND PURCHASERS
LEASES AND MORTGAGES
JOINT-STOCK COMPANIES
MASTERS, SERVANTS AND WORKMEN
CONTRACTS AND AGREEMENTS
MONEY LENDERS, SURETISHIP
PARTNERSHIP, SHIPPING LAW
SALE AND PURCHASE OF GOODS
CHEQUES, BILLS AND NOTES
BILLS OF SALE, BANKRUPTCY
LIFE, FIRE, AND MARINE INSURANCE
LIBEL AND SLANDER

CRIMINAL LAW
PARLIAMENTARY ELECTIONS
COUNTY COUNCILS
DISTRICT AND PARISH COUNCILS
BOROUGH CORPORATIONS
TRUSTEES AND EXECUTORS
CLERGY AND CHURCHWARDENS
COPYRIGHT, PATENTS, TRADE MARKS
HUSBAND AND WIFE, DIVORCE
INFANCY, CUSTODY OF CHILDREN
PUBLIC HEALTH AND NUISANCES
INNKEEPERS AND SPORTING
TAXES AND DEATH DUTIES

FORMS OF WILLS, AGREEMENTS, NOTICES, &C.

☞ *The object of this work is to enable those who consult it to help themselves to the law ; and thereby to dispense, as far as possible, with professional assistance and advice. There are many wrongs and grievances which persons submit to from time to time through not knowing how or where to apply for redress ; and many persons have as great a dread of a lawyer's office as of a lion's den. With this book at hand it is believed that many a* SIX-AND-EIGHTPENCE *may be saved ; many a wrong redressed ; many a right reclaimed ; many a law suit avoided ; and many an evil abated. The work has established itself as the standard legal adviser of all classes, and has also made a reputation for itself as a useful book of reference for lawyers residing at a distance from law libraries, who are glad to have at hand a work embodying recent decisions and enactments*

*** OPINIONS OF THE PRESS.

"The amount of information given in the volume is simply wonderful. The continued popularity of the work shows that it fulfils a useful purpose."—*Law Journal.*

"As a book of reference this volume is without a rival."—*Pall Mall Gazette.*

"No Englishman ought to be without this book."—*Engineer.*

"Ought to be in every business establishment and in all libraries."—*Sheffield Post.*

"The 'Concise Dictionary' adds considerably to its value."—*Westminster Gazette.*

"It is a complete code of English Law written in plain language, which all can understand. . . . Should be in the hands of every business man, and all who wish to abolish lawyers' bills."—*Weekly Times.*

"A useful and concise epitome of the law, compiled with considerable care."—*Law Magazine.*

"A complete digest of the most useful facts which constitute English law."—*Globe.*

"Admirably done, admirably arranged, and admirably cheap."—*Leeds Mercury.*

"A concise, cheap, and complete epitome of the English law. So plainly written that he who runs may read, and he who reads may understand."—*Figaro.*

"A dictionary of legal facts well put together. The book is a very useful one."—*Spectator*

LABOUR CONTRACTS.

A Popular Handbook on the Law of Contracts for Works and Services. By DAVID GIBBONS. Fourth Edition, with Appendix of Statutes by T. F. UTTLEY, Solicitor. Fcap. 8vo, cloth **3/6**

BRADBURY, AGNEW, & CO. LD., PRINTERS, LONDON AND TONBRIDGE.

WEALE'S SERIES

OF

SCIENTIFIC AND TECHNICAL

WORKS.

" It is not too much to say that no books have ever proved more popular with or more useful to young engineers and others than the excellent treatises comprised in WEALE'S SERIES."—**Engineer.**

A New Classified List.

Capio Lumen

CROSBY LOCKWOOD AND SON,

7, STATIONERS' HALL COURT, LONDON, E.C.

1904.

CIVIL ENGINEERING & SURVEYING.

Civil Engineering.
By HENRY LAW, M.Inst.C.E. Including a Treatise on HYDRAULIC ENGINEERING by G. R. BURNELL, M.I.C.E. Seventh Edition, revised, with LARGE ADDITIONS by D. K. CLARK, M.I.C.E. . . . **6/6**

Pioneer Engineering:
A Treatise on the Engineering Operations connected with the Settlement of Waste Lands in New Countries. By EDWARD DOBSON, M.INST.C.E. With numerous Plates. Second Edition **4/6**

Iron Bridges of Moderate Span:
Their Construction and Erection. By HAMILTON W. PENDRED. With 40 Illustrations **2/0**

Iron and Steel Bridges and Viaducts.
A Practical Treatise upon their Construction for the use of Engineers, Draughtsmen, and Students. By FRANCIS CAMPIN, C.E. With Illus. **3/6**

Constructional Iron and Steel Work,
As applied to Public, Private, and Domestic Buildings. By FRANCIS CAMPIN, C.E. **3/6**

Tubular and other Iron Girder Bridges.
Describing the Britannia and Conway Tubular Bridges. By G. DRYSDALE DEMPSEY, C.E. Fourth Edition **2/0**

Materials and Construction:
A Theoretical and Practical Treatise on the Strains, Designing, and Erection of Works of Construction. By FRANCIS CAMPIN, C.E. . . **3/0**

Sanitary Work in the Smaller Towns and in Villages.
By CHARLES SLAGG, Assoc. M.Inst.C.E. Third Edition . . **3/0**

Construction of Roads and Streets.
By H. LAW, C.E., and D. K. CLARK, C.E. Sixth Edition, revised, with Additional Chapters by A. J. WALLIS-TAYLER, A.M. Inst. C.E. . **6/0**

Gas Works,
Their Construction and Arrangement and the Manufacture and Distribution of Coal Gas. Originally written by S. HUGHES, C.E. Ninth Edition. Revised, with Notices of Recent Improvements, by HENRY O'CONNER, A.M. Inst. C.E., Author of "The Gas Engineers' Pocket Book."
[*Just Published.* **6/0**

Water Works
For the Supply of Cities and Towns. With a Description of the Principal Geological Formations of England as influencing Supplies of Water. By SAMUEL HUGHES, F.G.S., C.E. Enlarged Edition **4/0**

The Power of Water,
As applied to drive Flour Mills, and to give motion to Turbines and other Hydrostatic Engines. By JOSEPH GLYNN, F.R.S. New Edition . **2/0**

Wells and Well-Sinking.
By JOHN GEO. SWINDELL, A.R.I.B.A., and G. R. BURNELL, C.E. Revised Edition. With a New Appendix on the Qualities of Water. Illustrated **2/0**

The Drainage of Lands, Towns, and Buildings.
By G. D. DEMPSEY, C.E. Revised, with large Additions on Recent Practice, by D. K. CLARK, M.I.C.E. Third Edition . . . **4/6**

The Blasting and Quarrying of Stone,
For Building and other Purposes. With Remarks on the Blowing up of Bridges. By Gen. Sir J. BURGOYNE, K.C.B. **1/6**

Foundations and Concrete Works.
With Practical Remarks on Footings, Planking, Sand, Concrete Béton, Pile-driving, Caissons, and Cofferdams. By E. DOBSON. Ninth Ed. **1/6**

Pneumatics,
Including Acoustics and the Phenomena of Wind Currents, for the Use of Beginners. By CHARLES TOMLINSON, F.R.S. Fourth Edition . **1/6**

Land and Engineering Surveying.
For Students and Practical Use. By T. BAKER, C.E. Nineteenth Edition, Revised and Extended by F. E. DIXON, A.M. Inst. C.E., Professional Associate of the Institution of Surveyors. With numerous Illustrations and two Lithographic Plates **2/0**

Mensuration and Measuring.
For Students and Practical Use. With the Mensuration and Levelling of Land for the purposes of Modern Engineering. By T. BAKER, C.E. New Edition by E. NUGENT, C.E. **1/6**

MINING AND METALLURGY.

Mining Calculations,
For the use of Students Preparing for the Examinations for Colliery Managers' Certificates, comprising numerous Rules and Examples in Arithmetic, Algebra, and Mensuration. By T. A. O'DONAHUE, M.E., First-Class Certificated Colliery Manager. **3/6**

Mineralogy,
Rudiments of. By A. RAMSAY, F.G.S. Fourth Edition, revised and enlarged. Woodcuts and Plates **3/6**

Coal and Coal Mining,
A Rudimentary Treatise on. By the late Sir WARINGTON W. SMYTH, F.R.S. Eighth Edition, revised by T. FORSTER BROWN . '**3/6**

Metallurgy of Iron.
Containing Methods of Assay, Analyses of Iron Ores, Processes of Manufacture of Iron and Steel, &c. By H. BAUERMAN, F.G.S. With numerous Illustrations. Sixth Edition, revised and enlarged . . . **5/0**

The Mineral Surveyor and Valuer's Complete Guide.
By W. LINTERN. Fourth Edition, with an Appendix on Magnetic and Angular Surveying **3/6**

Slate and Slate Quarrying:
Scientific, Practical, and Commercial. By D. C. DAVIES, F.G.S. With numerous Illustrations and Folding Plates. Fourth Edition . . **3/0**

A First Book of Mining and Quarrying,
With the Sciences connected therewith, for Primary Schools and Self-Instruction. By J. H. COLLINS, F.G.S. Second Edition . . . **1/6**

Subterraneous Surveying,
With and without the Magnetic Needle. By T. FENWICK and T. BAKER, C.E. Illustrated **2/6**

Mining Tools.
Manual of. By WILLIAM MORGANS, Lecturer on Practical Mining at the Bristol School of Mines **2/6**

Mining Tools, Atlas
Of Engravings to Illustrate the above, containing 235 Illustrations of Mining Tools, drawn to Scale. 4to **4/6**

Physical Geology,
Partly based on Major-General PORTLOCK's "Rudiments of Geology." By RALPH TATE, A.L.S., &c. Woodcuts. **2/0**

Historical Geology,
Partly based on Major-General PORTLOCK's "Rudiments." By RALPH TATE, A.L.S., &c. Woodcuts **2/6**

Geology, Physical and Historical.
Consisting of "Physical Geology," which sets forth the Leading Principles of the Science; and "Historical Geology," which treats of the Mineral and Organic Conditions of the Earth at each successive epoch. By RALPH TATE, F.G.S. **4/6**

4 WEALE'S SCIENTIFIC AND TECHNICAL SERIES.

MECHANICAL ENGINEERING.

The Workman's Manual of Engineering Drawing.
By JOHN MAXTON, Instructor in Engineering Drawing, Royal Naval College, Greenwich. Eighth Edition. 300 Plates and Diagrams . **3/6**

Fuels: Solid, Liquid, and Gaseous.
Their Analysis and Valuation. For the Use of Chemists and Engineers. By H. J. PHILLIPS, F.C.S., formerly Analytical and Consulting Chemist to the Great Eastern Railway. Fourth Edition. **2/0**

Fuel, Its Combustion and Economy.
Consisting of an Abridgment of "A Treatise on the Combustion of Coal and the Prevention of Smoke." By C. W. WILLIAMS, A.I.C.E. With Extensive Additions by D. K. CLARK, M.Inst.C.E. Fourth Edition . **3/6**

The Boilermaker's Assistant
In Drawing, Templating, and Calculating Boiler Work, &c. By J. COURTNEY, Practical Boilermaker. Edited by D. K. CLARK, C.E. . **2/0**

The Boiler-Maker's Ready Reckoner,
With Examples of Practical Geometry and Templating for the Use of Platers, Smiths, and Riveters. By JOHN COURTNEY. Edited by D. K. CLARK, M.I.C.E. Fifth Edition **4/0**
⁎ *The last two Works in One Volume, half-bound, entitled* "THE BOILER-MAKER'S READY-RECKONER AND ASSISTANT." By J. COURTNEY and D. K. CLARK. *Price* **7/0**.

Steam Boilers:
Their Construction and Management. By R. ARMSTRONG, C.E. Illustrated **1/6**

Steam and Machinery Management.
A Guide to the Arrangement and Economical Management of Machinery. By M. POWIS BALE, M.Inst.M.E. **2/6**

Steam and the Steam Engine,
Stationary and Portable. Being an Extension of the Treatise on the Steam Engine of Mr. J. SEWELL. By D. K. CLARK, C.E. Fourth Edition **3/6**

The Steam Engine,
A Treatise on the Mathematical Theory of, with Rules and Examples for Practical Men. By T. BAKER, C.E. **1/6**

The Steam Engine.
By Dr. LARDNER. Illustrated **1/6**

Locomotive Engines.
By G. D. DEMPSEY, C.E. With large Additions treating of the Modern Locomotive, by D. K. CLARK, M.Inst.C.E. **3/0**

Locomotive Engine-Driving.
A Practical Manual for Engineers in charge of Locomotive Engines. By MICHAEL REYNOLDS. Eleventh Edition. 3s. 6d.; cloth boards . **4/6**

Stationary Engine-Driving.
A Practical Manual for Engineers in charge of Stationary Engines. By MICHAEL REYNOLDS. Seventh Edition. 3s. 6d.; cloth boards . **4/6**

The Smithy and Forge.
Including the Farrier's Art and Coach Smithing. By W. J. E. CRANE. Fourth Edition **2/6**

Modern Workshop Practice,
As applied to Marine, Land, and Locomotive Engines, Floating Docks, Dredging Machines, Bridges, Ship-building, &c. By J. G. WINTON. Fourth Edition, Illustrated **3/6**

Mechanical Engineering.
Comprising Metallurgy, Moulding, Casting, Forging, Tools, Workshop Machinery, Mechanical Manipulation, Manufacture of the Steam Engine, &c. By FRANCIS CAMPIN, C.E. Third Edition **2/6**

Details of Machinery.
Comprising Instructions for the Execution of various Works in Iron in the Fitting-Shop, Foundry, and Boiler-Yard. By FRANCIS CAMPIN, C.E. **3/0**

Elementary Engineering:
A Manual for Young Marine Engineers and Apprentices. In the Form of Questions and Answers on Metals, Alloys, Strength of Materials, &c. By J. S. BREWER. Fifth Edition **1/6**

Power in Motion:
Horse-power Motion, Toothed-Wheel Gearing, Long and Short Driving Bands, Angular Forces, &c. By JAMES ARMOUR, C.E. Third Edition **2/0**

Iron and Heat,
Exhibiting the Principles concerned in the Construction of Iron Beams, Pillars, and Girders. By J. ARMOUR, C.E. **2/6**

Practical Mechanism,
And Machine Tools. By T. BAKER, C.E. With Remarks on Tools and Machinery, by J. NASMYTH, C.E. **2/6**

Mechanics:
Being a concise Exposition of the General Principles of Mechanical Science, and their Applications. By CHARLES TOMLINSON, F.R.S. . . **1/6**

Cranes (The Construction of),
And other Machinery for Raising Heavy Bodies for the Erection of Buildings, &c. By JOSEPH GLYNN, F.R.S. **1/6**

NAVIGATION, SHIPBUILDING, ETC.

The Sailor's Sea Book:
A Rudimentary Treatise on Navigation. By JAMES GREENWOOD, B.A. With numerous Woodcuts and Coloured Plates. New and enlarged Edition. By W. H. ROSSER **2/6**

Practical Navigation.
Consisting of THE SAILOR'S SEA-BOOK, by JAMES GREENWOOD and W. H. ROSSER; together with Mathematical and Nautical Tables for the Working of the Problems, by HENRY LAW, C.E., and Prof. J. R. YOUNG . **7/0**

Navigation and Nautical Astronomy,
In Theory and Practice. By Prof. J. R. YOUNG. New Edition. **2/6**

Mathematical Tables,
For Trigonometrical, Astronomical, and Nautical Calculations; to which is prefixed a Treatise on Logarithms. By H. LAW, C.E. Together with a Series of Tables for Navigation and Nautical Astronomy. By Professor J. R. YOUNG. New Edition **4/0**

Masting, Mast-Making, and Rigging of Ships.
Also Tables of Spars, Rigging, Blocks; Chain, Wire, and Hemp Ropes, &c., relative to every class of vessels. By ROBERT KIPPING, N.A. . **2/0**

Sails and Sail-Making.
With Draughting, and the Centre of Effort of the Sails. By ROBERT KIPPING, N.A. **2/6**

Marine Engines and Steam Vessels.
By R. MURRAY, C.E. Eighth Edition, thoroughly revised, with Additions by the Author and by GEORGE CARLISLE, C.E. . . . **4/6**

Naval Architecture:
An Exposition of Elementary Principles. By JAMES PEAKE . . **3/6**

Ships for Ocean and River Service,
Principles of the Construction of. By HAKON A. SOMMERFELDT . **1/6**

Atlas of Engravings
. To Illustrate the above. Twelve large folding Plates. Royal 4to, cloth **7/6**

The Forms of Ships and Boats.
By W. BLAND. Tenth Edition, with numerous Illustrations and Models **1/6**

6   WEALE'S SCIENTIFIC AND TECHNICAL SERIES.

ARCHITECTURE AND THE BUILDING ARTS.

Constructional Iron and Steel Work,
As applied to Public, Private, and Domestic Buildings. By FRANCIS CAMPIN, C.E. **3/6**

Building Estates:
A Treatise on the Development, Sale, Purchase, and Management of Building Land. By F. MAITLAND. Third Edition **2/0**

The Science of Building:
An Elementary Treatise on the Principles of Construction. By E. WYNDHAM TARN, M.A. Lond. Fourth Edition **3/6**

The Art of Building:
General Principles of Construction, Strength, and Use of Materials, Working Drawings, Specifications, &c. By EDWARD DOBSON, M.R.I.B.A. . **2/0**

A Book on Building,
Civil and Ecclesiastical. By Sir EDMUND BECKETT, Q.C. (Lord GRIMTHORPE). Second Edition **4/6**

Dwelling-Houses (The Erection of),
Illustrated by a Perspective View, Plans, and Sections of a Pair of Villas, with Specification, Quantities, and Estimates. By S. H. BROOKS, Architect **2/6**

Cottage Building.
By C. BRUCE ALLEN. Twelfth Edition, with Chapter on Economic Cottages for Allotments, by E. E. ALLEN, C.E. **2/0**

Acoustics in Relation to Architecture and Building:
The Laws of Sound as applied to the Arrangement of Buildings. By Professor T. ROGER SMITH, F.R.I.B.A. New Edition, Revised . . **1/6**

The Rudiments of Practical Bricklaying.
General Principles of Bricklaying; Arch Drawing, Cutting, and Setting; Pointing; Paving, Tiling, &c. By ADAM HAMMOND. With 68 Woodcuts **1/6**

The Art of Practical Brick Cutting and Setting.
By ADAM HAMMOND. With 90 Engravings **1/6**

Brickwork:
A Practical Treatise, embodying the General and Higher Principles of Bricklaying, Cutting and Setting; with the Application of Geometry to Roof Tiling, &c. By F. WALKER **1/6**

Bricks and Tiles,
Rudimentary Treatise on the Manufacture of; containing an Outline of the Principles of Brickmaking. By E. DOBSON, M.R.I.B.A. Additions by C. TOMLINSON, F.R.S. Illustrated **3/0**

The Practical Brick and Tile Book.
Comprising: BRICK AND TILE MAKING, by E. DOBSON, M.INST.C.E.; Practical BRICKLAYING, by A. HAMMOND; BRICK-CUTTING AND SETTING, by A. HAMMOND. 550 pp. with 270 Illustrations, half-bound . . **6/0**

Carpentry and Joinery—
THE ELEMENTARY PRINCIPLES OF CARPENTRY. Chiefly composed from the Standard Work of THOMAS TREDGOLD, C.E. With Additions, and TREATISE ON JOINERY, by E. W. TARN, M.A. Eighth Edition . . **3/6**

Carpentry and Joinery—Atlas
Of 35 Plates to accompany and Illustrate the foregoing book. With Descriptive Letterpress. 4to **6/0**

A Practical Treatise on Handrailing;
Showing New and Simple Methods. By GEO. COLLINGS. Third Edition, including a TREATISE ON STAIRBUILDING. With Plates . . . **2/6**

Circular Work in Carpentry and Joinery.
A Practical Treatise on Circular Work of Single and Double Curvature. By GEORGE COLLINGS. Fourth Edition **2/6**

Roof Carpentry:
Practical Lessons in the Framing of Wood Roofs. For the Use of Working Carpenters. By GEO. COLLINGS **2/0**

The Construction of Roofs of Wood and Iron;
Deduced chiefly from the Works of Robison, Tredgold, and Humber. By E. WYNDHAM TARN, M.A., Architect. Fourth Edition . . . **1/6**

The Joints Made and Used by Builders.
By WYVILL J. CHRISTY, Architect. With 160 Woodcuts . . **3/0**

Shoring
And its Application: A Handbook for the Use of Students. By GEORGE H. BLAGROVE. With 31 Illustrations **1/6**

The Timber Importer's, Timber Merchant's, and Builder's Standard Guide.
By R. E. GRANDY **2/0**

Plumbing:
A Text-Book to the Practice of the Art or Craft of the Plumber. With Chapters upon House Drainage and Ventilation. By WM. PATON BUCHAN. Ninth Edition, with 512 Illustrations **3/6**

Ventilation:
A Text Book to the Practice of the Art of Ventilating Buildings. By W. P. BUCHAN, R.P., Author of " Plumbing," &c. With 170 Illustrations **3/6**

The Practical Plasterer:
A Compendium of Plain and Ornamental Plaster Work. By W. KEMP **2/0**

House Painting, Graining, Marbling, & Sign Writing.
With a Course of Elementary Drawing, and a Collection of Useful Receipts. By ELLIS A. DAVIDSON. Eighth Edition. Coloured Plates . . **5/0**
. The above, in cloth boards, strongly bound, **6/0**

A Grammar of Colouring,
Applied to Decorative Painting and the Arts. By GEORGE FIELD. New Edition, enlarged, by ELLIS A. DAVIDSON. With Coloured Plates **3/0**

Elementary Decoration
As applied to Dwelling Houses, &c. By JAMES W. FACEY. Illustrated **2/0**

Practical House Decoration.
A Guide to the Art of Ornamental Painting, the Arrangement of Colours in Apartments, and the Principles of Decorative Design. By JAMES W. FACEY **2/6**
. The last two Works in One handsome Vol., half-bound, entitled " HOUSE DECORATION, ELEMENTARY AND PRACTICAL," price **5/0**.

Portland Cement for Users.
By HENRY FAIJA, A.M.Inst.C.E. Third Edition, Corrected . . **2/0**

Limes, Cements, Mortars, Concretes, Mastics, Plastering, &c.
By G. R. BURNELL, C.E. Fifteenth Edition **1/6**

Masonry and Stone-Cutting.

The Principles of Masonic Projection and their application to Construction. By EDWARD DOBSON, M.R.I.B.A. **2/6**

Arches, Piers, Buttresses, &c.:

Experimental Essays on the Principles of Construction.   By W. BLAND. **1/6**

Quantities and Measurements,

In Bricklayers', Masons', Plasterers', Plumbers', Painters', Paperhangers', Gilders', Smiths', Carpenters' and Joiners' Work. By A. C. BEATON. **1/6**

The Complete Measurer:

Setting forth the Measurement of Boards, Glass, Timber and Stone. By R. HORTON. Sixth Edition **4/0**

Guide to Superficial Measurement:

Tables calculated from 1 to 200 inches in length, by 1 to 108 inches in breadth. For the use of Architects, Surveyors, Engineers, Timber Merchants, Builders, &c. By JAMES HAWKINGS. Fifth Edition . . **3/6**

Light:

An Introduction to the Science of Optics. For the Use of Students of Architecture, Engineering, and other Applied Sciences. By E. W. TARN, M.A. **1/6**

Hints to Young Architects.

By GEORGE WIGHTWICK, Architect. Sixth Edition, revised and enlarged by G. HUSKISSON GUILLAUME, Architect **3/6**

Architecture—Orders:

The Orders and their Æsthetic Principles. By W. H. LEEDS. Illustrated. **1/6**

Architecture—Styles:

The History and Description of the Styles of Architecture of Various Countries, from the Earliest Period. By T. TALBOT BURY . . **2/0**

₄ ORDERS AND STYLES OF ARCHITECTURE, *in One Vol.*, **3/6.**

Architecture—Design:

The Principles of Design in Architecture, as deducible from Nature and exemplified in the Works of the Greek and Gothic Architects. By EDW. LACY GARBETT, Architect. Illustrated **2/6**

₄ *The three preceding Works in One handsome Vol., half-bound, entitled* "MODERN ARCHITECTURE," *price* **6/0.**

Perspective for Beginners.

Adapted to Young Students and Amateurs in Architecture, Painting, &c. By GEORGE PYNE **2/0**

Architectural Modelling in Paper.

By T. A. RICHARDSON. With Illustrations, engraved by O. JEWITT **1/6**

Glass Staining, and the Art of Painting on Glass.

From the German of Dr. GESSERT and EMANUEL OTTO FROMBERG. With an Appendix on THE ART OF ENAMELLING **2/6**

Vitruvius—The Architecture of.

In Ten Books. Translated from the Latin by JOSEPH GWILT, F.S.A., F.R.A.S. With 23 Plates **5/0**

N.B.—This is the only Edition of VITRUVIUS *procurable at a moderate price.*

Grecian Architecture,

An Inquiry into the Principles of Beauty in. With an Historical View of the Rise and Progress of the Art in Greece. By the EARL OF ABERDEEN. **1/0**

₄ *The two preceding Works in One handsome Vol., half-bound, entitled* "ANCIENT ARCHITECTURE," *price* **6/0.**

INDUSTRIAL AND USEFUL ARTS.

Cements, Pastes, Glues, and Gums.
A Guide to the Manufacture and Application of Agglutinants. With 900
Recipes and Formulæ. By H. C. STANDAGE **2/0**

Clocks, Watches, and Bells for Public Purposes.
A Rudimentary Treatise. By EDMUND BECKETT, LORD GRIMTHORPE,
LL.D., K.C., F.R.A.S. Eighth Edition, with new List of Great Bells and
an Appendix on Weathercocks. [*Just published.* **4/6**
*** *The above, handsomely bound, cloth boards,* **5/6.**

Electro-Metallurgy,
Practically Treated. By ALEXANDER WATT. Tenth Edition . **3/6**

The Goldsmith's Handbook.
Containing full Instructions in the Art of Alloying, Melting, Reducing,
Colouring, Collecting and Refining, Recovery of Waste, Solders, Enamels,
&c., &c. By GEORGE E. GEE. Sixth Edition **3/0**

The Silversmith's Handbook,
On the same plan as the GOLDSMITH'S HANDBOOK. By G. E. GEE. **3/0**
*** *The last two Works, in One handsome Vol., half-bound,* **7/0.**

The Hall-Marking of Jewellery.
Comprising an account of all the different Assay Towns of the United
Kingdom ; with the Stamps and Laws relating to the Standards and Hall
Marks at the various Assay Offices. By GEORGE E. GEE . . **3/0**

French Polishing and Enamelling.
Numerous Recipes for making Polishes, Varnishes, &c. By R. BITMEAD.
1/6

Practical Organ Building.
By W. E. DICKSON, M.A. Second Edition, Revised, with Additions **2/6**

Coach-Building:
A Practical Treatise. By JAMES W. BURGESS. With 57 Illustrations **2/6**

The Cabinet-Maker's Guide
To the Entire Construction of Cabinet-Work. By R. BITMEAD . **2/6**

The Brass Founder's Manual:
Instructions for Modelling, Pattern Making, &c. By W. GRAHAM . **2/0**

The Sheet-Metal Worker's Guide.
For Tinsmiths, Coppersmiths, Zincworkers, &c. By W. J. E. CRANE. **1/6**

Sewing Machinery:
Its Construction, History, &c. By J. W. URQUHART, C.E. . . **2/0**

Gas Fitting :
A Practical Handbook. By JOHN BLACK. New Edition . . **2/6**

Construction of Door Locks.
From the Papers of A. C. HOBBS. Edited by C. TOMLINSON, F.R.S. **2/6**

**The Model Locomotive Engineer, Fireman, and
Engine-Boy.**
By MICHAEL REYNOLDS **3 6**

The Art of Letter Painting made Easy.
By J. G. BADENOCH. With 12 full-page Engravings of Examples . **1/6**

The Art of Boot and Shoemaking.
Measurement, Last-fitting, Cutting-out, Closing, &c. By J. B. LENO. **2/0**

Mechanical Dentistry:
By CHARLES HUNTER. Fourth Edition **3/0**

Wood Engraving.
A Practical and Easy Introduction to the Art. By W. N. BROWN . **1/6**

Laundry Management.
A Handbook for Use in Private and Public Laundries . . . **2/0**

AGRICULTURE, GARDENING, ETC.

Draining and Embanking:
A Practical Treatise. By Prof. JOHN SCOTT. With 68 Illustrations **1/6**

Irrigation and Water Supply:
A Practical Treatise on Water Meadows, Sewage Irrigation, Warping, &c.; on the Construction of Wells, Ponds, Reservoirs, &c. By Prof. JOHN SCOTT. With 34 Illustrations **1/6**

Farm Roads, Fences, and Gates:
A Practical Treatise on the Roads, Tramways, and Waterways of the Farm; the Principles of Enclosures; and the different kinds of Fences, Gates, and Stiles. By Prof. JOHN SCOTT. With 75 Illustrations . **1/6**

Farm Buildings:
A Practical Treatise on the Buildings necessary for various kinds of Farms, their Arrangement and Construction, with Plans and Estimates. By Prof. JOHN SCOTT. With 105 Illustrations **2/0**

Barn Implements and Machines:
Treating of the Application of Power and Machines used in the Threshing-barn, Stockyard, Dairy, &c. By Prof. J. SCOTT. With 123 Illustrations.
2/0

Field Implements and Machines:
With Principles and Details of Construction and Points of Excellence, their Management, &c. By Prof. JOHN SCOTT. With 138 Illustrations . **2/0**

Agricultural Surveying:
A Treatise on Land Surveying, Levelling, and Setting-out; with Directions for Valuing Estates. By Prof. J. SCOTT. With 62 Illustrations . **1/6**

Farm Engineering.
By Professor JOHN SCOTT. Comprising the above Seven Volumes in One, 1,150 pages, and over 600 Illustrations. Half-bound . . . **12/0**

Outlines of Farm Management.
Treating of the General Work of the Farm; Stock; Contract Work; Labour, &c. By R. SCOTT BURN **2/6**

Outlines of Landed Estates Management.
Treating of the Varieties of Lands, Methods of Farming, Setting-out of Farms, Roads, Fences, Gates, Drainage, &c. By R. SCOTT BURN. **2/6**

Soils, Manures, and Crops.
(Vol. I. OUTLINES OF MODERN FARMING.) By R. SCOTT BURN . **2/0**

Farming and Farming Economy.
(Vol. II. OUTLINES OF MODERN FARMING.) By R. SCOTT BURN **3/0**

Stock: Cattle, Sheep, and Horses.
(Vol. III. OUTLINES OF MODERN FARMING.) By R. SCOTT BURN **2/6**

Dairy, Pigs, and Poultry.
(Vol. IV. OUTLINES OF MODERN FARMING.) By R. SCOTT BURN **2/0**

Ut'lization of Sewage, Irrigation, and Reclamation of Waste Land.
(Vol. V. OUTLINES OF MODERN FARMING.) By R. SCOTT BURN . **2/6**

Outlines of Modern Farming.
By R. SCOTT BURN. Consisting of the above Five Volumes in One, 1,250 pp., profusely Illustrated, half-bound **12/0**

Book-keeping for Farmers and Estate Owners.
A Practical Treatise, presenting, in Three Plans, a system adapted for all
classes of Farms. By J. M. WOODMAN. Fourth Edition . . 2/6

Ready Reckoner for the Admeasurement of Land.
By A. ARMAN. Revised and extended by C. NORRIS. Fifth Edition 2/0

**Miller's, Corn Merchant's, and Farmer's Ready
Reckoner.**
Second Edition, revised, with a Price List of Modern Flour Mill Machinery,
by W. S. HUTTON, C.E. 2/0

The Hay and Straw Measurer.
New Tables for the Use of Auctioneers, Valuers, Farmers, Hay and Straw
Dealers, &c. By JOHN STEELE 2/0

Meat Production.
A Manual for Producers, Distributors, and Consumers of Butchers' Meat.
By JOHN EWART 2/8

Sheep:
The History, Structure, Economy, and Diseases of. By W. C. SPOONER,
M.R.V.S. Fifth Edition, with fine Engravings 3/6

Market and Kitchen Gardening.
By C. W. SHAW, late Editor of "Gardening Illustrated" . . 3/6

Kitchen Gardening Made Easy.
Showing the best means of Cultivating every known Vegetable and Herb,
&c., with directions for management all the year round. By GEORGE M. F.
GLENNY. Illustrated 1/6

Cottage Gardening:
Or Flowers, Fruits, and Vegetables for Small Gardens. By E. HOBDAY,
1/6

Garden Receipts.
Edited by CHARLES W. QUIN 1/6

Fruit Trees,
The Scientific and Profitable Culture of. From the French of M. Du
BREUIL. Fifth Edition, carefully Revised by GEORGE GLENNY. With
187 Woodcuts 3/6

The Tree Planter and Plant Propagator:
With numerous Illustrations of Grafting, Layering, Budding, Implements,
Houses, Pits, &c. By SAMUEL WOOD 2/0

The Tree Pruner:
A Practical Manual on the Pruning of Fruit Trees, Shrubs, Climbers, and
Flowering Plants. With numerous Illustrations. By SAMUEL WOOD 1/6
₊ *The above Two Vols. in One, handsomely half-bound, price* 3/6.

The Art of Grafting and Budding.
By CHARLES BALTET. With Illustrations 2/6

MATHEMATICS, ARITHMETIC, ETC.

Descriptive Geometry,
An Elementary Treatise on ; with a Theory of Shadows and of Perspective, extracted from the French of G. MONGE. To which is added a Description of the Principles and Practice of Isometrical Projection. By J. F. HEATHER, M.A. With 14 Plates **2/0**

Practical Plane Geometry :
Giving the Simplest Modes of Constructing Figures contained in one Plane and Geometrical Construction of the Ground. By J. F. HEATHER, M.A. With 215 Woodcuts **2/0**

Analytical Geometry and Conic Sections,
A Rudimentary Treatise on. By JAMES HANN. A New Edition, re-written and enlarged by Professor J. R. YOUNG . . . . **2'0**

Euclid (The Elements of).
With many Additional Propositions and Explanatory Notes ; to which is prefixed an Introductory Essay on Logic. By HENRY LAW, C.E. . .**2/6**
  ₊ *Sold also separately, viz :—*
Euclid. The First Three Books. By HENRY LAW, C.E. . . . **1/6**
Euclid. Books 4, 5, 6, 11, 12. By HENRY LAW, C.E. . . . **1/6**

Plane Trigonometry,
The Elements of. By JAMES HANN. **1/6**

Spherical Trigonometry,
The Elements of. By JAMES HANN. Revised by CHARLES H. DOW-LING, C.E. **1/0**
₊ *Or with " The Elements of Plane Trigonometry," in One Volume,* **2 6**

Differential Calculus, O
Elements of the. By W. S. B. WOOLHOUSE, F.R.A.S., &c. . . **1/6**

Integral Calculus.
By HOMERSHAM COX, B.A. **1/6**

Algebra,
The Elements of. By JAMES HADDON, M.A. With Appendix, containing Miscellaneous Investigations, and a Collection of Problems . . **2/0**

A Key and Companion to the Above.
An extensive Repository of Solved Examples and Problems in Algebra. By J. R. YOUNG **1/6**

Commercial Book-keeping.
With Commercial Phrases and Forms in English, French, Italian, and German. By JAMES HADDON, M.A. **1/6**

Arithmetic,
A Rudimentary Treatise on. With full Explanations of its Theoretical Principles, and numerous Examples for Practice. For the Use of Schools and for Self-Instruction. By J. R. YOUNG, late Professor of Mathematics in Belfast College. Thirteenth Edition **1/6**

A Key to the Above.
By J. R. YOUNG **1/6**

Equational Arithmetic,
Applied to Questions of Interest, Annuities, Life Assurance, and General Commerce ; with various Tables by which all Calculations may be greatly facilitated. By W. HIPSLEY **1/6**

Arithmetic,
Rudimentary, for the Use of Schools and Self-Instruction. By JAMES HADDON, M.A. Revised by ABRAHAM ARMAN **1/6**

A Key to the Above.
By A. ARMAN **1/6**

Mathematical Instruments:
Their Construction, Adjustment, Testing, and Use concisely Explained. By J. F. HEATHER, M.A., of the Royal Military Academy, Woolwich. Fifteenth Edition, Revised, with Additions, by A. T. WALMISLEY, M.I.C.E. Original Edition, in 1 vol., Illustrated **2/0**

* *In ordering the above, be careful to say "Original Edition," or give the number in the Series (32), to distinguish it from the Enlarged Edition in 3 vols. (as follows)—*

Drawing and Measuring Instruments.
Including—I. Instruments employed in Geometrical and Mechanical Drawing, and in the Construction, Copying, and Measurement of Maps and Plans. II. Instruments used for the purposes of Accurate Measurement, and for Arithmetical Computations. By J. F. HEATHER, M.A. . **1/6**

Optical Instruments.
Including (more especially) Telescopes, Microscopes, and Apparatus for producing copies of Maps and Plans by Photography. By J. F. HEATHER, M.A. Illustrated **1/6**

Surveying and Astronomical Instruments.
Including—I. Instruments used for Determining the Geometrical Features of a portion of Ground. II. Instruments employed in Astronomical Observations. By J. F. HEATHER, M.A. Illustrated. . . . **1/6**

* *The above three volumes form an enlargement of the Author's original work, "Mathematical Instruments," price* **2/0**. *(Described at top of page.)*

Mathematical Instruments:
Their Construction, Adjustment, Testing and Use. Comprising Drawing, Measuring, Optical, Surveying, and Astronomical Instruments. By J. F. HEATHER, M.A. Enlarged Edition, for the most part entirely re-written. The Three Parts as above, in One thick Volume. **4/6**

The Slide Rule, and How to Use It.
Containing full, easy, and simple Instructions to perform all Business Calculations with unexampled rapidity and accuracy. By CHARLES HOARE, C.E. With a Slide Rule, in tuck of cover. Eighth Edition . . **2/6**

Logarithms.
With Mathematical Tables for Trigonometrical, Astronomical, and Nautical Calculations. By HENRY LAW, C.E. Revised Edition . . **3/0**

Compound Interest and Annuities (Theory of).
With Tables of Logarithms for the more Difficult Computations of Interest, Discount, Annuities, &c., in all their Applications and Uses for Mercantile and State Purposes. By FEDOR THOMAN, Paris. Fourth Edition . **4/0**

Mathematical Tables,
For Trigonometrical, Astronomical, and Nautical Calculations ; to which is prefixed a Treatise on Logarithms. By H. LAW, C.E. Together with a Series of Tables for Navigation and Nautical Astronomy. By Professor J. R. YOUNG. New Edition **4/0**

Mathematics,
As applied to the Constructive Arts. By FRANCIS CAMPIN, C.E., &c. Third Edition **3/0**

Astronomy.
By the late Rev. ROBERT MAIN, F.R.S. Third Edition, revised and corrected to the Present Time. By W. T. LYNN, F.R.A.S. . . . **2/0**

Statics and Dynamics,
The Principles and Practice of. Embracing also a clear development of Hydrostatics, Hydrodynamics, and Central Forces. By T. BAKER, C.E. Fourth Edition **1/6**

BOOKS OF REFERENCE AND MISCELLANEOUS VOLUMES.

A Dictionary of Painters, and Handbook for Picture Amateurs.
Being a Guide for Visitors to Public and Private Picture Galleries, and for Art-Students, including Glossary of Terms, Sketch of Principal Schools of Painting, &c. By PHILIPPE DARYL, B.A. **2/6**

Painting Popularly Explained.
By T. J. GULLICK, Painter, and JOHN TIMBS, F.S.A. Including Fresco, Oil, Mosaic, Water Colour, Water-Glass, Tempera Encaustic, Miniature, Painting on Ivory, Vellum, Pottery, Enamel, Glass, &c. Sixth Edition **5/0**

A Dictionary of Terms used in Architecture, Building, Engineering, Mining, Metallurgy, Archæology, the Fine Arts, &c.
By JOHN WEALE. Sixth Edition. Edited by R. HUNT, F.R.S. . **5/0**

Music:
A Rudimentary and Practical Treatise. With numerous Examples. By CHARLES CHILD SPENCER **2/6**

Pianoforte,
The Art of Playing the. With numerous Exercises and Lessons. By CHARLES CHILD SPENCER **1/6**

The House Manager.
A Guide to Housekeeping, Cookery, Pickling and Preserving, Household Work, Dairy Management, Cellarage of Wines, Home-brewing and Wine-making, Gardening, &c. By AN OLD HOUSEKEEPER . . **3/6**

Manual of Domestic Medicine.
By R. GOODING, M D. Intended as a Family Guide in all cases of Accident and Emergency. Third Edition, carefully revised . . **2/0**

Management of Health.
A Manual of Home and Personal Hygiene. By Rev. JAMES BAIRD **1/0**

Natural Philosophy,
For the Use of Beginners. By CHARLES TOMLINSON, F.R.S. . . **1/6**

The Elementary Principles of Electric Lighting.
By ALAN A. CAMPBELL SWINTON, M.INST.C.E., M.I.E.E. Fifth Edition **1/6**

The Electric Telegraph,
Its History and Progress. By R. SABINE, C.E., F.S.A., &c. . . **3/0**

Handbook of Field Fortification.
By Major W. W. KNOLLYS, F.R.G.S. With 163 Woodcuts . . **3/0**

Logic,
Pure and Applied. By S. H EMMENS **1/6**

Locke on the Human Understanding,
Selections from. With Notes by S. H. EMMENS **1/6**

The Compendious Calculator
(*Intuitive Calculations*). Or Easy and Concise Methods of Performing the various Arithmetical Operations required in Commercial and Business Transactions ; together with Useful Tables, &c. By DANIEL O'GORMAN. Twenty-eighth Edition, carefully revised by C. NORRIS . . . **2/6**

Measures, Weights, and Moneys of all Nations.
With an Analysis of the Christian, Hebrew, and Mahometan Calendars.
By W. S. B. WOOLHOUSE, F.R.A.S., F.S.S. Seventh Edition . **2/6**

Grammar of the English Tongue,
Spoken and Written. With an Introduction to the Study of Comparative
Philology. By HYDE CLARKE, D.C.L. Fifth Edition. . . . **1/6**

Dictionary of the English Language.
As Spoken and Written. Containing above 100,000 Words. By HYDE
CLARKE, D.C.L. **3/6**

Composition and Punctuation,
Familiarly Explained for those who have neglected the Study of Grammar.
By JUSTIN BRENAN. Nineteenth Edition. **1/6**

French Grammar.
With Complete and Concise Rules on the Genders of French Nouns. By
G. L. STRAUSS, Ph.D. **1/6**

English-French Dictionary.
Comprising a large number of Terms used in Engineering, Mining, &c.
By ALFRED ELWES **2/0**

French Dictionary.
In two Parts—I. French-English. II. English-French, complete in
One Vol. **3/0**

French and English Phrase Book.
Containing Introductory Lessons, with Translations, Vocabularies of Words,
Collection of Phrases, and Easy Familiar Dialogues **1/6**

German Grammar.
Adapted for English Students, from Heyse's Theoretical and Practical
Grammar, by Dr. G. L. STRAUSS **1/6**

German Triglot Dictionary.
By N. E. S. A. HAMILTON. Part I. German-French-English. Part II.
English-German-French. Part III. French-German-English . . **3/0**

German Triglot Dictionary.
(As above). Together with German Grammar, in One Volume . **5/0**

Italian Grammar.
Arranged in Twenty Lessons, with Exercises. By ALFRED ELWES. **1/6**

Italian Triglot Dictionary,
Wherein the Genders of all the Italian and French Nouns are carefully
noted down. By ALFRED ELWES. Vol. I. Italian-English-French. **2/6**

Italian Triglot Dictionary.
By ALFRED ELWES. Vol. II. English-French-Italian . . . **2/6**

Italian Triglot Dictionary.
By ALFRED ELWES. Vol. III. French-Italian-English . . . **2/6**

Italian Triglot Dictionary.
(As above). In One Vol. **7/6**

Spanish Grammar.
In a Simple and Practical Form. With Exercises. By ALFRED ELWES **1/6**

Spanish-English and English-Spanish Dictionary.
Including a large number of Technical Terms used in Mining, Engineering,
&c., with the proper Accents and the Gender of every Noun. By ALFRED
ELWES **4/0**
₊ *Or with the* GRAMMAR, **6/0**.

Portuguese Grammar,
In a Simple and Practical Form. With Exercises. By ALFRED ELWES. **1/6**

Portuguese-English and English-Portuguese Dictionary.
Including a large number of Technical Terms used in Mining, Engineering, &c., with the proper Accents and the Gender of every Noun. By ALFRED ELWES. Fourth Edition, revised **5/0**
⁎ *Or with the* GRAMMAR, **7/0.**

Animal Physics,
Handbook of. By DIONYSIUS LARDNER, D.C.L. With 520 Illustrations. In One Vol. (732 pages), cloth boards **7/6**
⁎ *Sold also in Two Parts, as follows:—*
ANIMAL PHYSICS. By Dr. LARDNER. Part I., Chapters I.—VII. **4/0**
ANIMAL PHYSICS. By Dr. LARDNER. Part II., Chapters VIII.—XVIII. **3/0**

BRADBURY, AGNEW & CO., LD., PRINTERS, LONDON AND TONBRIDGE.
[96. 20.8]

www.ingramcontent.com/pod-product-compliance
Lightning Source LLC
Chambersburg PA
CBHW030608270326
41927CB00007B/1093